D1238106

IPAD®
QuickSteps®
Second Edition

JOLI BALLEW

New York Chicago San Francisco
Lisbon London Madrid Mexico City
Milan New Delhi San Juan
Seoul Singapore Sydney Toronto

The McGraw·Hill Companies

Cataloging-in-Publication Data is on file with the Library of Congress

McGraw-Hill books are available at special quantity discounts to use as premiums and sales promotions, or for use in corporate training programs. To contact a representative, please e-mail us at bulksales@mcgraw-hill.com.

IPAD® QUICKSTEPS®, SECOND EDITION

1234567890   QDB QDB   1098765432

ISBN   978-0-07-180371-7
MHID   0-07-180371-8

SPONSORING EDITOR / Megg Morin

EDITORIAL SUPERVISOR / Jody McKenzie

PROJECT MANAGER / Nidhi Chopra, Cenveo Publisher Services

ACQUISITIONS COORDINATOR / Stephanie Evans

TECHNICAL EDITOR / Janet Cloninger

COPY EDITOR / Lisa McCoy

PROOFREADERS / Julie Searls and Claire Splan

INDEXER / Valerie Haynes Perry

PRODUCTION SUPERVISOR / George Anderson

COMPOSITION / Cenveo Publisher Services

ILLUSTRATION / Cenveo Publisher Services

ART DIRECTOR, COVER / Jeff Weeks

COVER DESIGNER / Pattie Lee

SERIES CREATORS / Marty and Carole Matthews

SERIES DESIGN / Bailey Cunningham

For Allison; what a magical time to come into the world!

Acknowledgments

This book is a team effort of truly talented people.

Megg Morin, sponsoring editor, friend, and iPad enthusiast. Megg kept everyone in line, on track, and on time. Megg was always available, which is very important when pushing a book out quickly.

Janet Cloninger, my favorite technical editor in the entire world, who meticulously read and corrected my work, and did so quickly and precisely. She is truly awesome and incredibly knowledgeable.

Everyone who helped manage, shape, and create this book: **Stephanie Evans** and **Jody McKenzie** from McGraw-Hill, **Nidhi Chopra** and her production team from Cenveo Publisher Services, and **Lisa McCoy**, **Julie Searls**, **Claire Splan**, and **Valerie Haynes Perry**.

Neil Salkind, my agent, who goes out of his way to keep me busy. He's a great friend and my biggest fan. I'm sure I wouldn't be where I am today without him.

My family, who support my work and sincerely attempt to show enthusiasm at every turn and with every new gadget I drag home. They often let me slide when I'm immersed with it instead of the current conversation.

About the Author

Joli Ballew is an award-winning, best-selling technical author of more than 40 books. Joli has been working with computers, gadgets, and all things media since her freshman year in college in 1982, when she majored in computer science and system analysis, ultimately ending up with a degree in mathematics. Joli has written several books related to smart phones and mobile technologies, including the extremely popular *How to Do Everything: iPad 2* (McGraw-Hill) and *How to Do Everything: BlackBerry Storm2* (McGraw-Hill). Joli also teaches computer classes at various colleges in the Dallas area, and is the IT coordinator at Brookhaven College, part of the Dallas County community college system.

Beyond writing books and teaching classes, Joli is a Microsoft MVP and holds multiple Microsoft certifications, studies new technologies regularly, and attends both the Consumer Electronics Show and the Microsoft MVP Summit every year in order to keep up with the latest and greatest technologies. In her spare time, Joli exercises at her local gym, works outside tending to her manicured lawn, and serves as the butler for her two cats, Pico and Lucy, and their pet hamsters, Pookie 1 and Pookie 2.

You can contact Joli and post questions through her Facebook iPad group page, How to Do Everything: iPad. If you don't use Facebook, Joli welcomes your correspondence via e-mail at Joli_Ballew@hotmail.com.

About the Technical Editor

Janet Cloninger worked as a chemist and a programmer for many years before finding herself a work-at-home mom. Janet has written over 2,000 articles and product reviews for The Gadgeteer, a well-respected site for reviews of gadgets and gear. Her love of gadgets came from her father, who never met anything he couldn't fix or improve. Janet lives in North Carolina with her husband, Butch; her daughter, Rachel; and their shiba inu, Teddy.

Contents at a Glance

1 2 3 4 5 6 7 8 9 10

Contents

Chapter 4   **Using the Camera, Displaying Photos, Viewing Videos, and Exploring FaceTime** 51

Chapter 5   **Getting and Listening to Music and Audio** 69

4

5

Introduction

Congratulations on the purchase of your new iPad. You're going to be amazed at the media you can obtain and view, the books you can read, and how many ways you can stay in touch with others. You'll love surfing the Internet on a screen you can actually see; you'll appreciate Maps when you need to get somewhere fast or find information about a business or restaurant; and in your downtime, you'll enjoy shopping at the iTunes Store for movies, podcasts, music, TV shows, and just about any other media imaginable.

In this book you'll learn how to use all of the default apps that come with your iPad, how to acquire and use third-party apps, and how to incorporate iCloud and iTunes for backing up your data. You'll learn how to send iMessages, create reminders, and incorporate data that's stored on your home computers as well, among other things. You'll even learn how to stream your media across your home network.

There are a few things we won't cover though. We opted not to sign up for iTunes Match, an optional service from Apple that runs about $25 a year, and we don't have an Apple TV on our home network. We don't have any AirPort Express hardware either. If you have any of these, some of your screens will look a little different from ours. Similarly, we wrote the book with an iPad that has both Wi-Fi and cellular functions, so if your iPad is Wi-Fi only, you won't see the features or options related to cellular data. Don't worry, though—it's intuitive once you get into it, and we're sure this book will be the perfect fit for all readers!

We all sincerely hope that you are just as excited as we are about this new technology. We've tried to cover everything, but if you feel we've left anything out or if you have any questions or comments, feel free to e-mail me directly at joli_ballew@hotmail.com, or visit my Facebook group, How to Do Everything: iPad. It's open and everyone can join.

The QuickSteps Series

QuickSteps® books are recipe books for technology enthusiasts. They answer the question "How do I...?" by providing quick sets of steps to accomplish the most common tasks for the technology at hand. In addition, QuickSteps sidebars show you how to quickly do many small functions or tasks that support the primary functions. Notes, Tips, and Cautions augment the steps, yet they are presented in such a manner as to not interrupt the flow of the steps. The brief introductions are minimal rather than narrative, and numerous illustrations and figures, many with callouts, support the steps.

QuickSteps® books are organized by function and the tasks needed to perform that function. Each function is a chapter. Each task, or "How To," contains the steps needed for accomplishing the function along with relevant Notes, Tips, Cautions, and screenshots. Tasks will be easy to find through:

- The table of contents, which lists the functional areas (chapters) and tasks in the order they are presented

- A how-to list of tasks on the opening page of each chapter

- The index with its alphabetical list of terms used in describing the functions and tasks

- Color-coded tabs for each chapter or functional area with an index to the tabs just before the table of contents

Conventions Used in this Book

iPad® QuickSteps® uses several conventions designed to make the book easier for you to follow:

- A ⬤ or a ◍ in the table of contents or the how-to list in each chapter references a QuickSteps or a QuickFacts sidebar in a chapter.

- **Bold type** is used for words on the screen that you are to do something with, such as click **Save As** or open **File**.

- *Italic type* is used for a word or phrase that is being defined or otherwise deserves special emphasis.

- Underlined type is used for text that you are to type from the keyboard.

- When you see the command, **CTRL/CMD**, you are to press the **CTRL** key in Windows or the **CMD** key on the Mac; **ALT/OPT**, press the **ALT** key in Windows or the **OPTIONS** key on the Mac.

- SMALL CAPITAL LETTERS are used for keys on the keyboard such as **ENTER** and **SHIFT**.

- When you are expected to enter a command, you are told to press the key(s). If you are to enter text or numbers, you are told to type them. Specific letters or numbers to be entered will be underlined.

- When you are to click the mouse button on a screen command or menu, you will be told to "Click **File | Open**" which means, **"Click File**, then click **Open."**

How to...

Chapter 1

Getting Started

An iPad is a tablet computer designed, developed, and available from Apple that enables you to access the Internet, read e-books, upload and view pictures, watch movies, play games, and more from just about anywhere and at any time. It comes with its own apps too; a few are Calendar, Reminders, Maps, YouTube, and Newsstand. You can obtain additional apps from the App Store. You'll be able to enjoy your iPad and all of its apps after working through the initial setup process.

This chapter explains how to perform setup tasks and protect your iPad so that you can get the most from it right from the start. If you've already set up your iPad, don't worry; you can enable and disable features and settings easily, should you change your mind about anything after reading this chapter.

Set Up and Explore Your iPad

You have to set up your iPad before you can use it. You perform the setup tasks by working through a wizard that appears the first time you turn on your iPad. You've probably already done this. However, if you have not, or if you ever want to restore your iPad to factory settings and start over, you'll want to read the information in the next section.

Understand Your Setup Options

The first time you turn on your iPad (or after you've restored it to factory settings), you have to configure your iPad with your own, personal information, including the language you want to use, the network you want to connect to, your unique Apple ID, and more. You also need to decide how to set up your iPad, how to initially put your media on it, and whether or not to use iCloud.

If this is your first iPad, setup is pretty simple and doesn't require much time. You won't have very many decisions to make either. Once your iPad is set up, you'll use iTunes to transfer the data you have on your computer to your iPad if you desire, which enables you to put your personal data on it to populate it (music, pictures, videos, etc.). You'll use iTunes or iCloud similarly to back up the data you acquire on your iPad as you use it. If this is not your first iPad and you own (or have owned) another one; if you have purchased a new iPad to replace a stolen, lost, or broken one; or if you have some scenario similar to this, you have additional options. You can opt to set up your new iPad so it looks and acts like a new iPad, or you can make it look like your old iPad by syncing it with an existing backup from iTunes or iCloud. If these options exist, you can choose them during setup.

No matter which way you decide to go, you'll see that during the setup process, most of the options are easy to understand. You can easily choose a language or a network, or decide whether or not to use voice dictation. You won't need any help there. However, other prompts aren't so easy to understand. During setup,

TIP

The choices you make (or made) during setup aren't set in stone. You can always change your mind about how you use iCloud, how you've populated your iPad with data, and more.

you'll be asked to opt in or out of iCloud, choose how to initially populate your iPad with data (which can include syncing with a backup you already have in iTunes from a previous iPad), and to either input an existing Apple ID or get a new one.

Understand iCloud

iCloud is a new feature to iOS 5, the iPad's operating system. If you enable iCloud, you can use it to sync some of the data you keep on your iPad, including contacts, calendar data, reminders, Safari bookmarks, notes, and more, to Apple's Internet data servers. The first 5GB of data you save there is free. When data is synced to iCloud, you can access that data easily from all of your other iDevices. Likewise, data you save to iCloud on your other iDevices can be accessed from your iPad. iCloud also offers a handy way to back up specific kinds of data without syncing your iPad to your computer, and those backups happen automatically.

iCloud is extremely useful if you own more than one iDevice. For instance, if iCloud and Photo Stream are enabled on your iPad and your iPhone, when you take a picture on your iPhone, that picture will appear and be available from your iPad (and vice versa). You'll have to enable Photo Stream for this to work. If you enable Contacts in iCloud on specific iDevices and you change the e-mail address for a contact on one of them, that change will appear on the other iDevice automatically. This makes keeping your iDevices in sync simple.

However, you may not have additional iDevices. If you don't, you will probably still want to use iCloud. That's because iCloud can serve as a backup for your iPad. If your iPad, home computer, and personal backup device go missing, you can still access the data that was stored on your iPad from iCloud and restore that data to a new iPad should you decide to purchase a replacement. You can also restore from iCloud if your iPad must be restored to factory settings for any reason. No matter what you decide during setup, though, you can always change your mind later from Settings, shown in Figure 1-1.

TIP

To enable Photo Stream after you've set up your iPad, go to **Settings | Photos** and then opt to turn on Photo Stream.

TIP

No matter how you opt to set up your iPad, even if you want to depend on iCloud for your backups, we suggest you install iTunes on the computer you use most, as detailed next.

	iCloud	
.ıl... AT&T 🛜	9:28 AM	21% 🔋

Settings

	iCloud

iCloud

Account joliballew@gmail.com ＞

📧 Mail	OFF
👤 Contacts	ON
📅 Calendars	ON
📋 Reminders	ON
🔖 Bookmarks	ON
📒 Notes	ON
📷 Photo Stream	On ＞
📄 Documents & Data	On ＞
📍 Find My iPad	ON

Find My iPad allows you to locate this iPad on a map and remotely lock or erase it.

💾 Storage & Backup ＞

Delete Account

Settings list:
- ✈ Airplane Mode OFF
- 🛜 Wi-Fi 3802
- 🔔 Notifications
- 📍 Location Services On
- 📶 Cellular Data
- 🌅 Brightness & Wallpaper
- 🖼 Picture Frame
- ⚙ General
- ☁ iCloud
- ✉ Mail, Contacts, Calendars
- 🐦 Twitter
- 📹 FaceTime
- 🧭 Safari
- 💬 Messages
- 🎵 Music
- 🎬 Video

*Figure 1-1: **After you complete the setup process, you can configure how you want iCloud to work from Settings.***

Install iTunes

You need iTunes to manage and sync data between your computer and your iPad. Some things you may opt to sync are your media (including music, videos, movies, pictures, music videos, TV shows, podcasts, etc.), contacts, calendar appointments, and other data. You'll also use iTunes to back up and restore your iPad.

Even if you use iCloud and don't want to transfer any data from your computer to your iPad, because not every piece of data on your iPad can be stored in the cloud, iTunes is still important and is often a necessary backup strategy. However, when you use iTunes you want to make sure you don't sync the same thing to iTunes that you sync to iCloud, or problems may result. For instance, if you sync your contacts to iCloud and then also sync them with iTunes, you'll end up with duplicate entries as well as entries that conflict with others.

To download, install, and set up iTunes and obtain an iTunes Store account on a Windows-based PC (the steps for a Mac are similar but not exactly the same):

1. From your computer, visit www.apple.com/itunes/download.
2. Verify whether you want to leave the two options selected to receive e-mail notifications from Apple (and if so, provide your e-mail address). If you do not want to receive e-mail from Apple, deselect these items.

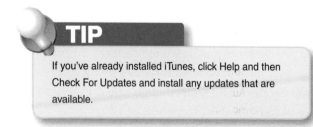

TIP

If you've already installed iTunes, click Help and then Check For Updates and install any updates that are available.

TIP

If you do not see the Set Up Your iPad screen, connect your iPad to your computer and/or click iPad in the left pane of iTunes.

TIP

Don't opt to sync all of your data if you have a lot of media and/or other iDevices. You probably don't want all of it on your iPad. You'll learn how to personalize the sync process in the next section.

NOTE

You may be prompted that certain music, audiobooks, or other media can't be copied. Make sure to read these carefully and resolve them. As an example, in the case of Audible (a popular audiobook store), you must authorize the iPad to access Audible data from it. In another scenario, music can't be copied due to copyright rules applied to it.

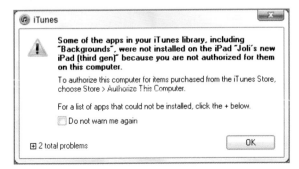

Figure 1-2: *Read the messages you encounter during setup, and resolve those problems as prompted.*

3. Click **Download Now**. If you are prompted to run or save the file, select Run.

4. Click **Next** to get started.

5. Configure installation options, including whether or not you want a shortcut to iTunes placed on your desktop and to use iTunes as the default player for audio files. Do not change the location of the iTunes folder unless you know what you're doing!

6. Click **Install**. You may have to provide administrator credentials or otherwise allow the installation on your computer.

7. Leave **Open iTunes After the Installer Exits** selected. Click **Finish**.

8. Click **Agree** to accept the software license agreement from Apple.

9. If prompted, click **Install** and/or **Finish**.

10. When iTunes starts, you'll be required to complete the rest of the setup process. This may involve connecting your iPad to your computer using the Universal Serial Bus (USB) cable that was included with it, waiting for a device driver to be installed, or creating an iTunes account. Follow the prompts to complete the process.

11. Once you see the Set Up Your iPad screen, you're ready to complete the setup process.

The steps for setting up your iPad in iTunes, either as a new iPad or from backup, will vary depending on the situation. So, instead of listing steps that will only apply in specific circumstances, here we'll simply point out some screens you may see along the way:

● You may have to select I Have Read And Agree To The iPad Software License Agreement (and you may actually want to read these).

● You may have to type your Apple ID and password, or work through the required process to create one.

● If you are registering your iPad, you will need to answer the required questions and click Submit.

● You will have to choose whether to set your iPad up as a new iPad, or use data you have as a backup.

● You will have to type a name for your iPad, and if desired, change the default options.

● You may have to click Store and then click Authorize This Computer if error messages appear during the first computer-to-iPad sync. See Figure 1-2.

TIP

You can set up syncing to occur automatically over Wi-Fi, when your iPad is connected to your home network and plugged in to a wall outlet, and when iTunes is running on your computer. You configure this option under the Summary tab.

TIP

If you have duplicate songs in your Music folder, they will be copied to your iPad. If you have duplicate contacts in your contact list, the same holds true. It's best to clean up your computer before syncing your iPad.

Explore Sync Options

The last part of the setup process involves syncing. Syncing is the process of copying data from your computer to your iPad and back again as data changes. You can sync data, pictures, music, movies, calendar appointments, contacts, e-books, and more. The first time you perform a sync, you'll mostly be copying data from your computer to your iPad. Afterward, each time you sync, you'll match up data between the two so that the same data is available on both, and the data on your computer will serve as a backup for your iPad. In addition, once syncing is configured, backups occur automatically. You can configure syncing now or later, but we suggest you set up syncing now.

To get started, connect your iPad to your computer using the supplied USB cable. Make sure to click your iPad in the left pane of iTunes. See Figure 1-3.

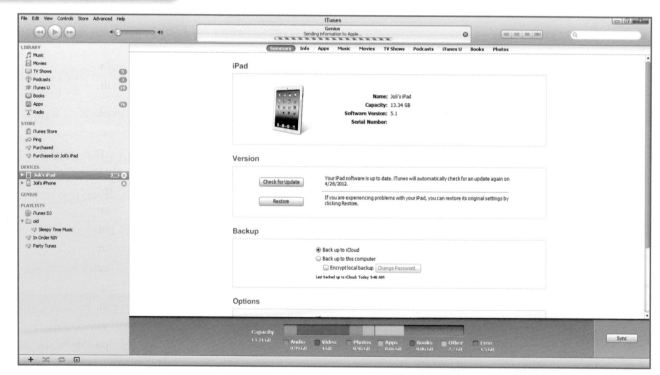

Figure 1-3: *You may see your other iDevices in the left (navigation) pane; select your iPad here.*

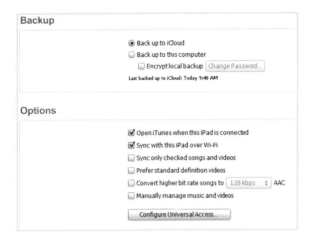

SUMMARY

Click the Summary tab to choose whether to back up to iCloud or not, to encrypt your local backup and assign a password to it, to sync your iPad over Wi-Fi when applicable, and more. If you have a Wi-Fi network, consider enabling Sync With This iPad Over Wi-Fi. When you do, you no longer have to physically connect your iPad to your computer to sync it, although your iPad will need to be connected to your Wi-Fi network and plugged in to a wall outlet to sync automatically (and iTunes will need to be running on the computer).

INFO

Click the Info tab to sync contacts, calendars, mail accounts (minus your passwords and messages), bookmarks, and notes with the information on your computer. If you use iCloud for any of these, don't enable them here. No matter what you opt to sync, if you make changes on your iPad, during the next sync, changes will be copied to your computer (and vice versa). Heed all warnings; a familiar warning is shown in Figure 1-4.

Choose to sync mail if you don't want to set up your e-mail accounts on your iPad manually but would instead rather copy (sync) the information from your computer. You can also keep Internet Explorer Favorites or Safari Bookmarks on your computer synced with the bookmarks on your iPad (but remember you can sync bookmarks with iCloud instead). Sync notes to copy notes you create on your iPad to your computer and vice versa, provided you have a compatible notes program on your desktop computer.

Figure 1-4: **Don't sync data to iCloud and your computer; problems will ensue.**

Summary Info **Apps** Music Movies TV Shows Podcasts iTunes U Books Photos

☑ **Sync Apps** Joli's iPad 42 apps

Sort by Kind ⬦

iPhone, iPod touch, and iPad Apps

☑ ▸**Solitaire**
Games 22.8 MB

☑ **ABC Player**
Entertainment 35.5 MB

☐ **Amazon Mobile**
Lifestyle 9.2 MB

☐ **American Airlines**
Travel 12.6 MB

☑ **AniMatch: Animal Pairs...**
Games 10.1 MB

☐ **Atari's Greatest Hits**
Games 21.9 MB

☑ **Blackboard Mobile™ Le...**
Education 18 MB

☐ **CLIPish Free - Millions...**
Social Networking 6.6 MB

☐ **Countdown to an Event**
Utilities 6.8 MB

☐ **Cut the Rope: Holiday...**
Games 21.6 MB

☐ **Doodle Jump: HOP The...**

☑ Automatically sync new apps

Select apps to be installed on your iPad or drag to a specific home screen.
Drag to rearrange app icons or home screens.

NOTE

Other tabs are available in iTunes, and some will appear only after you've obtained a specific type of data. As you acquire data, look for additional tabs, including iTunes U, TV Shows, and Books.

☑ **Sync Movies**

☐ Automatically include all

Movies

☑ **Avatar (2009)**
⏱ 161 minutes
2.35 GB
PG-13

APPS

You can redownload any app you get for free or purchase from the App Store from the App Store's Purchased tab, as you'll learn in Chapter 6. You can also opt to sync apps in iTunes. Syncing apps with iTunes enables you to save the data you've collected while using the app. Also, if you don't have automatic downloads of purchased apps on both your computer and your iPad, syncing apps can copy apps purchased on your iPad to the computer and vice versa. When you opt to sync apps, you can reposition the apps on your iPad using your computer. Here, we're dragging the Newsstand app to the next iPad screen using iTunes, and apps are set to sync.

MUSIC

Click the Music tab to sync all music or only specific artists, playlists, genres, or albums. You can also opt to sync music videos, voice notes, or to automatically fill free space on your iPad with songs. To see how much space your entire music library would require of your iPad, click **Entire Music Library**, and look at the **Capacity** bar that runs across the bottom of the screen. If you have more music than will fit on your iPad (or if you don't want all of it on there), you'll need to choose what you want to sync.

| Capacity 13.34 GB | Audio 7.3 GB | Video 4 GB | Photos 0.98 GB | Apps 0.86 GB | Books 0.06 GB | Other 2.2 GB | ⚠ Over Capacity by 1.85 GB | Revert / Apply |

MOVIES

Click the Movies tab to see what, if any, movies on your computer can be synced to your iPad. If you have quite a few movies on your computer, you probably can't sync them all because you won't have enough room on your iPad to store them. Click **Sync Movies**, but do not select **Automatically Include**. Then, select only the movies you want to sync to your iPad.

QUICKSTEPS

CONFIGURING iTUNES

You'll learn about syncing throughout this book in various chapters and in Chapter 9; however, you will want to sync some things now to get some data on your iPad. You can sync data using iTunes while your iPad is connected to your computer. With iTunes open and your iPad connected, look at each of the tabs and consider the options. If you're comfortable doing so, select some data now to sync and click Apply; if you aren't yet ready, you can wait for specific instructions on selecting data later in the book. You're safe selecting some photos and some music, though; you can't go wrong there.

QUICKFACTS

USING iCLOUD WITH MULTIPLE DEVICES

If you have an iPhone, iPad, and perhaps even an iPod touch, you may have a confusing mix of iTunes and iCloud syncing options configured. It is often best to review your settings on your devices, especially when you acquire a new one, and decide what you want to share among all of them. You may want to share contacts and calendar information, reminders, and notes, for instance, but you may not want to share bookmarks or photos.

To get started, first verify that each of your iDevices has the most up-to-date software on it, and then open Settings, then iCloud, and configure all of your devices to match. Turn on what you want to sync to iCloud and share among them all, and turn off what you don't. You can then opt to sync what's turned off with your computer (or not).

PHOTOS

Click the Photos tab to sync photos. Click **Sync Photos From** to see how much space syncing all photos in a specific folder will consume on your iPad. Since some videos also appear in various picture folders on your computer, select **Include Videos** if desired. It's likely that you can sync all of your photos, provided you leave Include Videos deselected.

APPLY

After you've selected a bit of data to sync (copy) to your iPad, click **Apply**. The sync will occur, and the selected data will be copied to your iPad. You'll see a new icon on the information bar that runs across the top of your iPad—a small, rotating circle—to show that syncing is taking place.

Explore the Outside of the iPad

Now that you're all set up and synced, let's look at the outside of the iPad. Several buttons and connections are available. With the screen facing toward you, there's a 30-pin docking port that allows you to charge your iPad or connect it to your computer, located just under the Home button. You'll also have access to a stereo headphone mini-jack, a switch to mute the volume or lock the screen rotation, and more. The list here is complete; while reading through it, locate each of these on your own iPad.

With the screen facing toward you and while holding the iPad in portrait mode, carefully turn your iPad in all directions and look for the following ports and features:

- **Home button** The small round button on the front of the iPad near the bottom. Use it to access the Lock screen when the iPad is inactive, to access the Home screen when the iPad is in use, and to perform other tasks outlined in this book.

- **30-Pin Dock Connector** The dock connector is located on the bottom of the iPad. This is where you connect accessories, such as the battery charger, docking stations, the Camera Connection Kit (optional), and other devices.

2

3

4

5

6

7

8

9

10

The iPad is only meant to be associated with one computer at a time. Syncing the iPad with a different computer than the one used for setup could result in loss of data.

 NOTE

If you haven't used the iPad for a few minutes, it'll lock itself automatically. You can lengthen or shorten the auto-lock duration by opening the Settings app, tapping General, and tapping the Auto-Lock option.

 TIP

When a number appears on an icon, it means new data is available (such as an update for an app or new mail).

- **Built-in Speaker** The speaker is behind the grid on the bottom right of the iPad, under the Home button, on the right side.
- **3.5 mm Stereo Headphone Mini-Jack** A standard headphone jack that accepts generic headphones and headsets is located at the top of the iPad on the left.
- **Microphone** The pinhole microphone is located on the top of the iPad, in the center, just above the front-facing camera lens.
- **Silent/Screen Rotation Lock** This lock is located on the right side of the iPad near the top, just above the volume buttons. Slide this switch to silence the iPad. You can change the function of this lock in the Settings app, from the General tab, to serve as a screen rotation lock instead.
- **Volume** The Volume rocker is located on the right side of the iPad underneath the Silent/Screen Rotation Lock. To use it, tap the top part to raise the volume and the bottom to lower it. Tap and hold the bottom part of the Volume rocker to mute the iPad quickly.
- **Sleep/Wake and On/Off** The Sleep/Wake button is located on the top of the iPad on the right; just apply a short press. You can use this button to turn on or off the iPad as well; apply a long press and hold, and then opt to turn off the iPad when prompted.
- **Camera Lenses** The front- and rear-facing camera lenses are at the top of their respective sides of the iPad.
- **Micro-SIM Card Tray** If you have a compatible iPad, this tray is located at the top, on the left side. You'll need a SIM eject tool (or a paperclip) to gain access.

Explore the Home Screen

The Lock screen is what you see when you turn on or access your iPad after it's been asleep or turned off (or when you stop playing a Picture Frame slideshow). This is a safeguard to keep it from being inadvertently enabled when not in use. Once you've used the slider to access the iPad, what you see is the Home screen. This screen gives you one-tap access to everything that's available on it. Later in this chapter you'll learn how to personalize this screen by moving the icons, and how to add or remove icons to make the iPad uniquely yours. For now, you'll want to explore what's on the Home screen already and learn to navigate around in it. The Home screen icons you'll want to familiarize yourself with are shown in Figure 1-5. You can create up to 11 Home screens.

Figure 1-5: *The iPad's Home screen offers one-tap access to the apps on it.*

The icons you'll see on the Home screen when you first turn it on include

- **Messages**   A messaging app you can use to send text and media messages to others who also have an iDevice. Devices you can send messages to include anyone with an iPhone, iPad, or iPod touch running iOS 5. If you're texting over Wi-Fi, it's free and unlimited too; text messaging rates do not apply.

- **Calendar**   A fully functional calendar that allows you to create and manage events; configure reminders for events; view the calendar by day, week, month, year, and lists of events; and add new calendars by incorporating applications like Microsoft Office Outlook or Google Calendar.

- **Notes**   An application that allows you to take notes easily. The Notes app looks like a yellow lined legal pad and allows you to create notes with a virtual keyboard and then e-mail them, delete them, print them using a compatible printer, or save them for future reference.

- **Reminders**   A to-do list application. With it you can dictate tasks you want to complete, tap those tasks to manage them, set audio reminders when a task is almost due, and even create multiple task lists. You might keep an ongoing shopping list here, for example.

- **Maps**   A full-fledged application for getting directions to local restaurants or points of interest; contacts' physical addresses; your current position (where you are); and for showing traffic, satellite views, typed directions, and more.

- **YouTube**   An application that allows you to quickly view YouTube video content, watch the most popular videos of the day, and search for videos you want to view. With YouTube, you can also mark your favorite videos so you can access them later or view similar videos easily. This is an app, though, and doesn't take you to the actual website.

- **Videos**   An application for managing the videos you own and watching videos you get from iTunes.

- **Contacts**   An application you use to manage the contacts you create or add. You can easily add new or edit existing contacts, select a contact to communicate with, or share contact information with others.

- **Game Center**   Game Center makes it easy to find games, play games, and create an online gaming identity and keep track of the games you play and the scores you earn, among other things.

- **iTunes**   An application that allows you to preview and purchase music and media on your iPad. (As with some of the other apps, you need to be online to access the iTunes Store.) Note that the iTunes app on the iPad is only a storefront and does not handle media management and playback as iTunes on a computer does.

- **App Store**   The App Store is where you purchase and download apps, including those that enable you to engage in social networking, manage your finances, obtain additional information about products you plan to buy, play games, share data, and more. Think of anything you'd like to do with your iPad; there's likely an app for that.

- **Newsstand**   This app holds magazines you purchase. To get a magazine, open Newsstand, visit the Newsstand portion of the App Store, and download the app for the magazine you want to read. When you return to Newsstand, you can then purchase those magazines easily.

- **Settings**   An application that enables you to turn on and off Wi-Fi; change sounds, brightness, and wallpaper; configure e-mail, contacts, and calendar options; change Safari defaults; change Music defaults, and more.

- **FaceTime**   FaceTime lets you hold video conversations with anyone else using a new iPad, iPad 2, iPhone 4, new iPod touch, or Mac over Wi-Fi, and any iDevices newer than these that include FaceTime. It works just as you'd expect a "video phone" to work, by assisting you in placing a call to a contact, initiating and holding a video conversation, and hanging up when your call is complete.

- **Photo Booth**   Photo Booth can be used to take pictures and apply effects to those pictures using either the front or rear camera lenses.

- **Camera**   The Camera app offers access to the front- and rear-facing cameras, enabling you to take both photos and video.

Figure 1-6: *Four default icons appear on the Dock, but these can be changed, and the Dock can hold up to six icons.*

TIP

Tap any icon one time to open its associated app. Tap the Home button (the round button on the front of the iPad) to return to the Home screen. You can also use five fingers to squeeze inward while in any app to return to the Home screen.

There are also four icons located across the bottom of the screen, on the Dock, shown in Figure 1-6:

- **Safari** A web browser for surfing the Internet. With it you can create bookmarks, set a home page, and perform common tasks associated with the Internet.

- **Mail** A complete e-mail solution. With Mail, you can send and receive e-mail, save and manage e-mail, and perform common tasks associated with e-mailing.

- **Photos** An application for viewing and managing photos. With Photos, you can view slideshows, browse your photos, perform simple editing, and even upload photos from a digital camera or media card (provided you purchase the Apple Camera Connection Kit). If you use iCloud, you can access photos stored there as well.

- **Music** A complete music player that enables you to play and manage music. You can create playlists of your favorite songs or access playlists that have been synced from your home computer too, like Most Played. You can also access files stored on your iPad or in iCloud (if you are using Apple's iTunes Match service).

Learn Touch Techniques

You need to know the names of the components and iPad-related words to understand the description of the navigation techniques. Most importantly, the items on the Home screen are called *icons,* and you *tap* or *touch* the icons to open their respective *apps.* When you open an app and tap in an area where you can type, the *virtual keyboard* appears. Tap the *keyboard icon* on the virtual keyboard to make the keyboard disappear. The keyboard is shown here.

QUICKSTEPS

USING TOUCH TECHNIQUES

There are plenty of ways to navigate your iPad with touch techniques or to use touch techniques to personalize it. Try the following techniques.

REPOSITION HOME SCREEN ICONS AND CREATE NEW HOME SCREENS

Tap and hold any icon on the Home screen, and when the icons start to jiggle, let go. Tap and hold any icon, and then drag it to a different area of the screen to reposition it. To move an icon off the current screen to another, drag it to the left or right side of the screen. When the new screen appears, let it go to move it there. Press the **Home** button to apply changes.

FLICK TO A NEW HOME SCREEN

If you've created new Home screens, you can flick to the new screens easily. To explore the available screens, from the default Home screen, lightly touch an area of the Home screen that is not covered with an app, and drag your finger to the right. This enables you to access the Spotlight search screen. Repeat and drag your finger left to return to the default Home screen, and then repeat to see additional screens you've created.

DRAG TO CREATE A FOLDER

Tap and hold any icon on any screen, and when the icons start to jiggle, drag one icon on to the top of a similar icon and let it go. When the new folder appears, tap the **X** in the new window to rename the folder. Press **Done** and then tap outside the new folder to return to the previous screen. Press the **Home** button once to apply. (To change it back, repeat these steps and drag the icons out of the folder to the screen.)

Continued . . .

In addition, there are various techniques beyond simply tapping:

- A *double-tap* is often used to zoom in on something like a photo or webpage.
- A *double-press* on the Home button opens up a small window that offers access to apps that are open and are available for use. Flick to move through them. You can also tap and hold on the apps that appear to access an option to close them.

- A *pinch* with your thumb and forefinger (either by pinching outward or inward) on a photo, webpage, or other compatible media is used to zoom in and out.
- A *tap-and-hold* action on an icon causes the icons to "jiggle." You can then rearrange them on the screen by keeping your finger on an icon and *dragging* it to a new area or screen. You can also tap the X that appears on any jiggling third-party app to delete it. You tap the Home button to stop the icons from "jiggling."
- A *flick,* sometimes called a *swipe,* is used to move from the Home screen to any other screen you've created (and back). A flick is a quick motion in which you move your finger quickly from one side of the screen to another, or from top to bottom. Flick right from your default Home screen to access the Spotlight search screen; flick left to return. Flick up or down to move quickly through data that is longer than one page, such as the contacts in your Contacts app or information on a webpage. You can also flick left and right to move to a new page in an e-book.

- After tapping and holding to make your icons "jiggle," *dragging* one icon on top of another enables you to create a new *folder.* Move similar apps into folders to organize them.

TIP

To quickly zoom in on a webpage, photo, or other compatible item, double-tap the screen. You can then double-tap again to zoom back out.

TIP

Once you have photos on your iPad, you can use them for wallpaper. Until that time you'll have to choose from the wallpaper that comes with your iPad.

- Tapping works within apps in various ways, too. Tap twice in a video to view it in full-screen mode, and tap twice again to return to regular viewing; tap once on text to access menus such as Select, Select All, Copy, and Paste; and tap once in an app like iBooks to show or hide controls.

- You can also use various multitasking gestures. You can use a five-finger inward pinching motion to exit an app and return to the Home screen. You can use a four-finger upward swipe to open the small window at the bottom of the screen that shows your currently running apps, and then a four-finger downward swipe to close that window. With any app open, you can use a four-finger swipe right and left to page through all of the active apps (those that appear in the small window at the bottom of the screen, when it's active). These multitasking gestures must be turned on from Settings | General | Multitasking Gestures.

Personalize Your iPad

You can personalize your iPad in ways other than repositioning icons or creating folders. You can change the wallpaper, change under what circumstances sounds are played, and create a passcode that must be input before you can use your iPad. The latter can protect your iPad from unauthorized use. Along those same lines, you can also protect your iPad with a feature currently called *Find My iPad*, which enables you to locate your iPad via global positioning system (GPS) if it's ever lost or stolen.

Change the Wallpaper on Your iPad

The picture on the Home screen is called the *wallpaper*. You can change the wallpaper to any picture you can get onto your iPad via syncing or other means, any you've taken with the camera, or any that Apple has provided for you (and there are several). If you don't have any of your own pictures yet, that's okay. You can always return here to set your favorite image as wallpaper when you do.

You can also assign a picture to the Lock screen. That's the image you see when the screen is locked but the display is on. In other words, it's the picture you see on the page that shows the slider to unlock the iPad before using it.

Figure 1-7: *You can access a lot of options from Settings, including Brightness & Wallpaper.*

To change the wallpaper for the Home screen, the Lock screen, or both:

1. On the Home screen, tap **Settings**.

2. In the Settings page, tap **Brightness & Wallpaper**. See Figure 1-7.

3. In the right pane, tap the arrow next to Wallpaper. (You can actually tap anywhere in the white box showing the two current screens.)

4. If you have pictures on your iPad, you'll see them in the resulting screen. If you do not have your own pictures yet, you'll only see the Wallpaper option. Tap any folder to view the pictures in it. Any other folders shown below Wallpaper are your own personal photos you've synced or imported.

5. If you see a picture you like, tap it, and tap one of the following options:

   a. **Set Lock Screen**   This is the screen you see when the computer is locked.

   b. **Set Home Screen**   This is the image you see on the Home screen, under the Home screen icons.

   c. **Set Both**   This shows the image on both screens.

   d. **Cancel**   This option returns you to the previous screen.

6. To return to the Settings window, tap **Back**, and then tap **Wallpaper**. You can, alternatively, click the **Home** button on the iPad.

Configure Sounds

Sounds play when you get new mail, send mail, get a Calendar alert, lock the iPad, or tap a key on the keyboard. Sounds also play at a level you've set using the Volume Rocker on the outside of the iPad. You can opt not to play any or all of these sounds inside the Settings app (and change the volume there too).

1. Tap **Settings**.

2. Tap **General**.

3. Tap **Sounds**.

TIP

If you created an additional Home screen page, you may have to flick left or right to find the Settings icon.

NOTE

Settings will open to the exact place you were the last time you used the Settings app. You can either tap whatever "back" button is available to return to a previous set of settings or simply tap an item in the left pane.

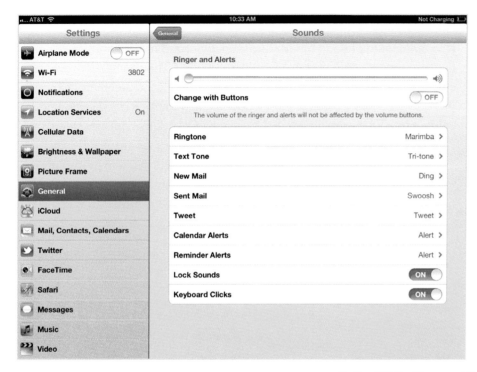

4. To change the Ringtone setting, tap **Marimba** and tap a new sound.

5. To turn on and off sounds for specific events, tap the **On** (or **Off**) button for any sound option to change it. You can also preview any sound by turning the sound for the event off and then back on. To understand what each of these options means, refer to the bulleted list, next.

6. Move the slider to change the volume.

The various sound options are

- **Ringtone**   The sound that plays when a FaceTime call arrives. Marimba, the default, is a light, ten-note song that repeats until you answer the call. You can hear it by tapping **Ringtone**, which opens a page with more options, and then **Marimba**.

- **Text Tone**   The sound that plays when a new messages arrives in the Messages app.

- **New Mail**   The sound that plays when a new e-mail arrives in the Mail app. The sound is a bright, short "ding" sound that plays one time.

TIP

You can also use the volume buttons to change the sound as it occurs, if you have turned on the Change With Buttons option under the slider in Sounds.

TIP

You don't have to "save" changes you make in the Settings app or tap any "back" button to apply them. Changes are applied immediately with no further input required from you.

- **Sent Mail**   The sound that plays when e-mail has been successfully sent. The sound that accompanies it is a "whoosh" sound that plays one time.

- **Tweet**   The sound that plays when you receive a new tweet.

- **Calendar Alerts**   The sound that plays when a calendar entry you've configured with specific criteria in conjunction with a reminder have been met. It sounds like a high-pitched siren and plays twice.

- **Reminder Alerts**   The sound that plays when a reminder is configured to notify you of a task.

- **Lock Sounds**   The sound that plays when you lock your iPad. It sounds like a camera when taking a picture. It plays one time. You can only turn this on or off.

- **Keyboard Clicks**   The sound that occurs when you tap a key on the keyboard. It's a short, low, staccato sound. A sound plays each time you tap a key. You can only turn this on or off.

CAUTION

You won't increase security if you lock the iPad after a specific amount of idle time but do not apply a passcode lock. Without a passcode lock, you only need to move the slider to unlock the iPad.

Use Auto-Lock and Passcode Lock

It's important to protect your iPad from unauthorized use. Without precautions in place, anyone could pick up your iPad and use it. This means they could send e-mail as you, listen to your media and watch your videos, and more. You can protect your iPad by configuring it to lock automatically after a specific amount of idle time and by applying a four-digit passcode lock that must be entered before the iPad can be used again. For even more security you can change the settings to allow an alphanumeric password and require a passcode immediately after waking the iPad.

To enable Auto-Lock and Passcode Lock:

1. Tap **Settings** and tap **General**. The General window opens, shown in Figure 1-8.
2. Tap **Auto-Lock**.
3. Tap the desired number of minutes.
4. Click **General** to return to the previous screen.
5. Tap **Passcode Lock** and then tap **Turn Passcode On**.
6. Type a four-digit passcode, and then repeat the code.
7. Tap the arrow next to **Require Passcode**.
8. Choose how much time should pass before a passcode is required.
9. Tap **Passcode Lock** to return to the previous screen.

Figure 1-8: The General window offers access to Auto-Lock, Passcode Lock, and more.

TIP

You can also opt to lock the iPad after a specific amount of time to increase battery life.

While configuring Passcode Lock, look at the other options, specifically Simple Passcode. If you turn off the Simple Passcode option, you can enter longer, more complex passcodes. It does not have to be a four-digit number. Note also the Erase Data option. If you enable this option, all of the data on the iPad will be erased after ten failed passcode attempts.

Enable Find My iPad

You can protect your iPad with a feature called Find My iPad. You enable it by selecting **Settings | iCloud** and then moving the slider for Find My iPad from Off to On. (You'll have to enable iCloud if you haven't yet done that.) Find My iPad offers the following features:

- It helps you locate your iPad if you lose or misplace it. Once Find My iPad has been enabled, should your iPad ever be misplaced, you can visit www.icloud.com to get its approximate location, provided the iPad is powered on.

- You can display a message on your iPad to help someone return it to you if it's lost.

- The Remote Passcode Lock feature lets you remotely lock your iPad. If your iPad is stolen while it is unlocked, you can easily lock it.

- The Remote Wipe feature lets you erase all content and settings on your iPad if it's stolen. This resets all settings to their original value and erases all your information, data, and media.

Once enabled, to try out Find My iPad:

1. Place your iPad in another room in your home or office.

2. From any computer, visit www.icloud.com.

3. Type your Apple ID and password.

4. Click **Sign In**.

5. Click **Find My iPhone** (or, perhaps, **Find My iPad**).

6. If you have multiple iDevices, select your iPad.

7. Note the location, and then click the small, blue i (Figure 1-9).

8. Click **Play Sound Or Send Message**.

9. Type <u>Where is my iPad?</u> and click **Send**.

10. Go and get your iPad and click **OK**.

*Figure 1-9: **Find your iPad at www.icloud.com, and click the blue i to access additional options.***

How to...

Chapter 2

Accessing and Surfing the Internet

The Internet provides easy access to worldwide information and news; local directions and maps; social networking sites; and music, video, and games, among other things. For many, having easy access to the Internet is the main reason for purchasing an iPad.

This chapter explains how to access and use the Internet from your iPad and get the most from it. You'll learn the difference between Wi-Fi and cellular data and how to connect to the Internet with either; how to use Safari, a web browser included on your iPad, to surf the Internet once connected; and how to save bookmarks, use Safari's new Reader, and configure Safari to keep you safe while you're online.

UNDERSTANDING Wi-Fi AND CELLULAR DATA

There are two different networking models for the iPad. The first is Wi-Fi only, and the second is Wi-Fi + 4G. (If you aren't in the U.S or Canada, your model may be called Wi-Fi + Cellular instead.)

Wi-Fi ONLY

The iPad Wi-Fi model connects to the Internet only one way: when you are within range of and have permission to use a Wi-Fi network. You may have a Wi-Fi network in your home or at work, and you can locate free Wi-Fi networks, called *hotspots,* in coffee shops, hotels, libraries, and similar establishments. You must be within range of a Wi-Fi network to get Internet access. There is no other way to get online.

Wi-Fi + 4G

The iPad Wi-Fi + 4G model connects to the Internet in two ways. One is through a Wi-Fi connection, described in the previous paragraph. The other is through a 4G (or other compatible) connection available via cellular networks. If you have a Wi-Fi + 4G model, you can get online at free Wi-Fi hotspots, your wireless network at work and at home, and, when those aren't available, using a cellular network. Note that you have to pay for a 4G data plan to obtain cellular access.

Connect to the Internet

Every iPad is capable of connecting to the Internet over a Wi-Fi network. If you have a Wi-Fi + 4G model iPad, you can connect to the Internet in two ways. You can connect to the Internet through an Internet-enabled Wi-Fi network, or you can connect via a cellular data plan you pay for each month. Free public Wi-Fi networks are available in coffee shops, libraries, hotels, and the like, and personal Wi-Fi networks are available in homes and businesses, and are often protected with a password. When a Wi-Fi network isn't available, and if you have a compatible iPad and data plan, you can connect to the Internet using a cellular data plan. Figure 2-1 shows the iPad connected to a Wi-Fi network and Safari open to the *New York Times* home page.

Figure 2-1: *Once connected to the Internet, you can surf the Web with Safari.*

TIP

Wi-Fi must be enabled to see and connect to wireless networks like the one in your home or your local library.

TIP

If you have a cellular data plan, leave Wi-Fi enabled at all times. This will ensure that you'll be connected to (or prompted to join) a Wi-Fi network when Wi-Fi is available. This will help limit your cellular data usage.

NOTE

Wi-Fi connections are almost always faster than 4G (or even Long-Term Evolution, LTE)—another reason to opt for Wi-Fi when it's available.

Connect to a Wi-Fi Network

To connect to a Wi-Fi network, your iPad's Wi-Fi feature must be enabled. When Wi-Fi is enabled, the iPad will constantly search for networks to connect to and will prompt you when one is within range. Once you've connected to any Wi-Fi network, the next time you're within range you'll be connected automatically. Also, you can forget any network you don't want to rejoin.

To connect to an available network:

1. If a Wi-Fi network is available, and if your iPad is configured to prompt you when it finds available wireless networks, when prompted to join a network:

   a. Tap the prompt.

   b. Tap **Join**.

2. To manually check for available wireless networks:

   a. Tap the **Settings** icon, and tap **Wi-Fi**.

   b. Under Choose A Network, tap any network to join it, as shown in Figure 2-2. (If you see a blue check by a network, you're already connected to it.)

3. If prompted, enter the password and tap **Join**.

4. Tap the **Home** button to return to the Home screen.

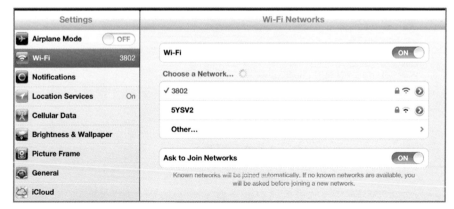

Figure 2-2: *You can view available wireless networks.*

Monitor Cellular Data Usage

If you have a Wi-Fi + 4G iPad and pay for a data plan from a provider like AT&T, you can access the Internet from anywhere, at any time, provided you're within their service range. If you choose the plan that only allows a small amount of data usage per month, you'll want to watch just how often you use the 4G (or compatible cellular) service; but if you have a more generous plan, there's less need to worry about usage.

UICKSTEPS

ENABLING NETWORK CONNECTIONS

Your iPad's Wi-Fi feature must be enabled to connect to wireless networks. Likewise, your iPad's Wi-Fi + 4G Cellular Data feature must be enabled to connect using your cellular data plan. If you're having problems viewing and joining networks, make sure that the features you need are indeed enabled. You can also enable LTE, which lets you surf the Web faster but uses more battery power. There are separate options for cellular data and LTE.

ENABLE WI-FI

1. From the Home screen, tap **Settings**.
2. In the left pane, tap **Wi-Fi**.
3. Move the Wi-Fi slider to **On**.

4. To be notified when Wi-Fi networks are available, move the Ask To Join Networks slider to **On**.
5. Tap the **Home** button to return to the Home screen.

ENABLE CELLULAR DATA

1. From the Home screen, tap **Settings**.
2. From the left pane, tap **Cellular Data**.
3. Move the Cellular Data slider to **On**.
4. To enable LTE, move the Enable LTE slider to **On**.
5. To enable data roaming, move the Data Roaming slider to **On**.
6. Tap the **Home** button to return to the Home screen.

You will want to disable the Cellular Data feature anytime you are away from a Wi-Fi network and don't want Mail and other apps to retrieve data or check for updates when you don't need them to. Some apps receive data from the Internet routinely, like social networking apps that get status updates behind the scenes or news apps that you configure or allow to offer pop-ups about breaking news. If you don't need to view these updates and are keeping an eye on your data usage, you can disable the Cellular Data feature when you aren't using the iPad. It's important to note, though, that some apps require Internet access to work, and disabling access may be problematic.

To see how much data you've used during your current cellular data billing cycle or to change your data plan:

1. Tap **Settings**.
2. Tap **Cellular Data**.
3. Tap **View Account**. See Figure 2-3.
4. Sign in as applicable and follow the prompts to view your account information.

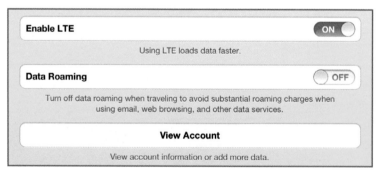

Figure 2-3: *You can keep track of your data usage by viewing your account information.*

CAUTION

You will likely be charged extra from your cellular data provider when roaming. Thus, it's best to leave the Data Roaming feature turned off. If you're told you're out of range (perhaps out of the country) and you choose to roam, you can enable this feature then.

TIP

You can turn off any app's ability to obtain updates automatically or obtain information automatically from Settings. This enables you to control how an individual app accesses or retrieves information from the Internet. See Chapter 10 for more information about Settings options.

Use Safari

Safari is the web browser that comes preinstalled on your iPad, and you use it to surf the Internet. It's a full browser; with it you can locate anything on the Web, view just about any webpage, view lots of types of web media, save and manage bookmarks for websites you visit often, and more. (You can even share a link via Twitter!) There are two views: Landscape and Portrait; you can zoom in and out of a page easily; and you can have multiple webpages open at once and switch among them with just a couple of taps with your finger.

As with other web browsers you've used, Safari offers easy-to-recognize icons, keeps track of the websites you've visited in the past, and when you type in a web address, offers addresses that start with the letters you've typed. If you see what you want in the resulting list, you can tap the suggestion to go there. You can also add icons for webpages you visit often right on the Home screen or the Bookmarks Bar, which you'll learn about later in this chapter. Safari is shown in Figure 2-4.

The Bookmarks icon lets you easily access saved bookmarks

The Add Bookmark icon lets you save webpage references

The Address window is where you type a webpage address

The Reload/Refresh button lets you reload any open webpage

Use the Back and Forward buttons to move among previously viewed webpages

The Search window is used to search for anything on the Internet

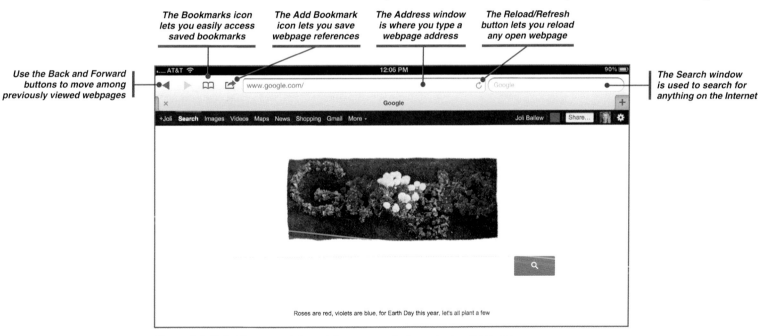

Figure 2-4: Safari is a complete web browser and offers plenty of features.

TIP

Safari is available from the Home screen by default, and is one of the four icons displayed across the bottom of the screen on the Dock.

NOTE

Before you can use Safari to surf the Web, you have to be connected to the Internet.

Visit a Webpage

There are several ways you can visit a webpage:

- Type the address of the webpage in the Address window. The address is called a Uniform Resource Locator (URL).

www.facebook.com/home.php

- Tap a link in a webpage. "Link" is short for *hyperlink*, and it offers one-tap access to another webpage. Most hyperlinks are blue.

up to 4G LTE. So you can o, and browse the web at Learn more ›

- Tap any bookmark on the Bookmarks Bar or in the Bookmarks list. A bookmark offers one-tap access to a page you visit often. (You'll learn more about bookmarks later in this chapter.)

- Tap the **Back** or **Forward** buttons when applicable. The Back and Forward buttons are only active after you've visited a few webpages.

- Tap a URL in a contact card, e-mail, document, or other medium. URLs are often called webpages.

To navigate to a webpage using the Address window:

1. Tap **Safari** on the Home screen.
2. Tap the Address window.
3. Tap the **X** in the Address window to clear any existing URLs.
4. Type <u>mcgrawhill</u> and tap the **.com** key.
5. Tap **Go**.

Perform a Search

The Search window in Safari offers an easy way to search for anything on the Internet. To perform a search, you simply tap inside the window, and when the virtual keyboard appears, type your keywords. If what you're looking for appears underneath, tap it to see the results. If not, click **Search** on the keyboard. Figure 2-5 shows an example.

Go to this address

TIP

Safari will automatically insert the "http://" and the "**www.**" if you don't type it.

NOTE

All websites offer links to other webpages. Click any link to navigate to a different webpage.

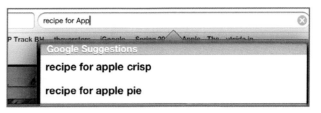

Figure 2-5: The Search window offers suggestions as you type.

View Media

Media you find on the Web will generally consist of pictures, videos, and music. Most of the time, you only need tap the media to view it or hear it. You can't view all of the media on the Web, however, because you can't view media that uses Adobe Flash. That's a limitation, but many (if not most) websites are now offering their videos without this requirement.

Some apps are designed specifically for viewing certain types of media, too. For instance, if you have a Netflix subscription, you can view the "Watch Instantly" movies that Netflix offers using its free Netflix app. If you missed your favorite television show on ABC, the ABC Player app lets you watch it on your iPad. HBO, Showtime, and others have similar apps. There are even apps that will "show you," with video, how to cook a recipe or perform first aid, among other things. You can also access instructional videos on the Web.

QUICKSTEPS

LOCATING AND VIEWING MEDIA

1. Tap **Safari** and navigate to www.apple.com.

2. If applicable, click the **iPad** tab at the top of the page.

3. In the iPad webpage, scroll down until you see an image with the Play arrow on it and tap it.

4. You may have to tap another Play button to play the video.

5. While the video plays, tap to access the video controls. If nothing happens, tap one or two more times.

6. Tap the controls as desired, noting the options to Pause and View Full Screen.

7. Tap the **Back** button to return to the previous page.

Incorporate Touch Techniques

You interact with Safari using one or two fingers. You can tap, pinch, and flick to access media, zoom in and out, and scroll, among other things. You may remember these terms from Chapter 1. In addition, you can easily switch from Portrait to Landscape mode by rotating your iPad 90 degrees left or right, and you can flip the iPad to turn the page upside-down, perhaps to show the page to a person sitting across from you.

The most common navigational touch techniques are

- **Tap (Touch)** to use the Back and Forward buttons, navigate to new webpages through links, go to any page you've bookmarked (which you may not have done yet), bring up the keyboard in any window that allows you to type in it, and more.

- **Pinch** to zoom in or out on any webpage, picture, or video.

- **Flick** to scroll through a page that runs longer than the length of the screen.

- **Rotate** or **Flip** rotate the iPad 90 degrees to switch from Portrait to Landscape mode or Landscape to Portrait mode, or flip it completely over to show the page to a person sitting across from you.

- **Four-finger swipe** left or right to move from Safari to another running app.

- **Five-finger inward pinch** to access the Home screen.

- **Four-finger up or down swipe** to show and hide the multitasking toolbar.

Use Bookmarks

A bookmark is a shortcut to a webpage you visit often or would like to find easily later. There's already at least one bookmark, a link to the iPad User Guide, saved there. Bookmarks appear in the Bookmarks list, available with a single tap after you tap the Bookmarks icon (see Figure 2-6). There are other options as well: *Reading list*, which holds webpages that contain articles you've marked that you'd like to read later; *History*, which offers a list of websites you've recently visited; and *Bookmarks Bar*, which contains bookmarks you save and want displayed at the top of your browser window for easy access. You can create your own "folders" too, including ones you see here (News, Travel) as well as your own bookmarks.

ZOOMING, SCROLLING, AND GETTING BACK TO THE TOP OF THE PAGE

Practice these touch techniques in Safari to see how they are applied in this medium.

PINCH TO ZOOM

On any webpage, put your thumb and forefinger together and pull them outward to zoom in on the webpage. You can zoom in or out on a picture or text, too. If a video is playing, you can use the pinching motion to switch from the current, smaller webpage view to full-screen view. Use a reverse pinching motion to zoom back out of any text, picture, webpage, or video.

FLICK TO SCROLL

On any webpage that is longer than the length of the screen, flick from the bottom of the page up to scroll down the page. Flick from the top of the page down to scroll up the page.

TOUCH THE iPAD STATUS BAR TO GET TO THE TOP OF A PAGE QUICKLY

If you've scrolled down the page, tap at the top of the screen (perhaps above the Address window) to return to the top of a webpage quickly.

TIP

If you have navigated to an article you'd like to read later but don't want to create a bookmark, tap Add To Reading List instead of Add Bookmark.

The Bookmarks icon displays bookmarks you've saved and those that have been included for you

The Edit button enables you to rearrange and delete bookmarks

Reading List lets you access articles you've marked to read later

History lets you access recently visited sites

The Bookmarks Bar offers a list of bookmarks you've specifically saved to this folder

Figure 2-6: **Tap the Bookmarks icon to access the Reading list, Bookmarks list, History, and the items in the Bookmarks Bar.**

To make sites you visit regularly easier to access, you can add a bookmark for them in the Bookmarks list. To add a bookmark to the Bookmarks list:

1. Tap **Safari** and navigate to the page for which you'd like to add a bookmark.

2. Tap the **Add Bookmark** icon, and tap **Add Bookmark**.

3. If desired, use the keyboard to type a new name.

TIP

If you're an avid Internet Explorer user, a bookmark is the same as a favorite.

TIP

Create a web clip on your Home screen for websites you access often, such as social networking sites, a blog you write, or web-based e-mail.

TIP

You can view the Bookmarks Bar by tapping the Address window. To show the Bookmarks Bar permanently, from the Home screen, tap **Settings**, tap **Safari**, and move the Always Show Bookmarks Bar slider to **On**, as detailed later.

TIP

Consider creating a Bookmark folder named Travel, and put links to all of your favorite travel-related websites there. Create additional folders named Help Pages, Apple, Job Hunting, Real Estate, or any other thing to organize other bookmarks you want to keep.

4. Verify that **Bookmarks** is selected. If the Bookmarks Bar is displayed instead (or something else), tap **Bookmarks Bar** (or the appropriate "back" button) and then tap **Bookmarks**.

5. Tap **Save**.

If there's a website you visit often, you can put an icon for that webpage on your Home screen. This is called a *web clip*. It gives you one-tap access to the page.

To save a webpage as a web clip:

1. Tap **Safari** and navigate to your favorite webpage.
2. Tap the **Add Bookmark** icon.
3. Tap **Add To Home Screen**.
4. If desired, change the name offered, and then tap **Add**.
5. Note the new icon.

To add a bookmark to the Bookmarks Bar and then view that bookmark:

1. Tap **Safari** and navigate to a favorite webpage.
2. Tap the **Add Bookmark** icon.
3. Tap **Add Bookmark**.
4. If desired, change the name offered.
5. Verify that **Bookmarks Bar** is showing; if not, tap whatever is, and tap **Bookmarks Bar**.
6. Tap **Save**.
7. To view the new bookmark, tap inside the Address window to show the Bookmarks Bar, and then tap the new bookmark.

Use Bookmark Folders

Finally, you can organize the bookmarks you keep in bookmark folders you create. This is often a better solution than simply having a single, long list of bookmarks, a cluttered Bookmarks Bar, or a Home screen filled with web clips.

CREATING BOOKMARK FOLDERS AND ADDING BOOKMARKS

Bookmark folders can be created in two places: the Bookmarks list and the Bookmarks Bar.

CREATE A BOOKMARK FOLDER IN THE BOOKMARKS LIST

To create a new bookmark folder on the Bookmarks list:

1. Tap the **Bookmarks** icon on the toolbar.

2. Tap **Edit**.

3. Tap **New Folder**.

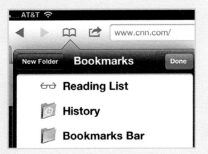

4. Type a name for the folder.

5. Verify that **Bookmarks** is displayed. (If something else is displayed instead, tap it.)

6. Tap **Bookmarks**.

7. Tap **Done**.

CREATE A BOOKMARK FOLDER IN THE BOOKMARKS BAR

To create a new bookmark folder on the Bookmarks Bar:

1. Tap the **Bookmarks** icon on the toolbar.

2. Tap **Edit**.

3. Tap **New Folder**.

Continued . . .

You can create these folders on the Bookmarks Bar or in the Bookmarks list. When saving bookmarks, you can save them to these folders easily.

Use the Reader and Reading List

The Add Bookmark icon on the navigation pane in Safari offers the option Add To Reading List. You use this option when you want to mark something you'd like to read later but don't want to create a bookmark for. When you are ready to read it, from the Bookmarks icon, you simply tap Reading List and select the item from it.

To mark an article for reading later:

1. Navigate to the page that contains the material you want to mark.

2. Tap the **Add Bookmark** icon.

3. Tap **Add To Reading List**.

To read the article later:

1. Tap the **Bookmark** icon.

2. Tap **Reading List**.

3. Tap **All** or **Unread**, as desired.

4. Tap the article you want to read.

Configure Settings to Stay Safe Online

You can change settings and preferences related to Safari for a better browsing experience from Settings on the Home screen. You can configure preferences, including what search engine to use; whether or not to automatically fill in web forms with your name, address, and the like; and whether or not you want to show the Bookmarks Bar permanently in Safari.

Safari helps you maintain your safety and privacy while on the Internet too. Settings that Safari deems optimal are already set, but it's always a good idea to review them. You can also clear your history, cookies, and cache, among other things. Safari's settings are shown in Figure 2-7.

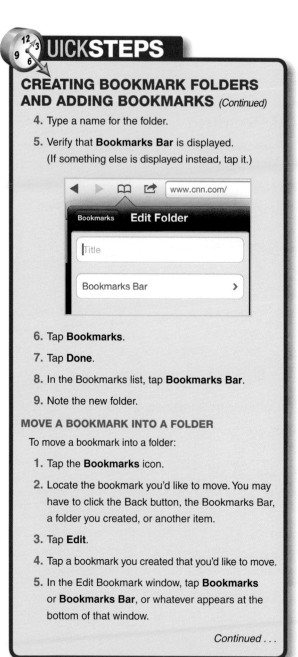

CREATING BOOKMARK FOLDERS AND ADDING BOOKMARKS *(Continued)*

4. Type a name for the folder.

5. Verify that **Bookmarks Bar** is displayed. (If something else is displayed instead, tap it.)

6. Tap **Bookmarks**.

7. Tap **Done**.

8. In the Bookmarks list, tap **Bookmarks Bar**.

9. Note the new folder.

MOVE A BOOKMARK INTO A FOLDER

To move a bookmark into a folder:

1. Tap the **Bookmarks** icon.

2. Locate the bookmark you'd like to move. You may have to click the Back button, the Bookmarks Bar, a folder you created, or another item.

3. Tap **Edit**.

4. Tap a bookmark you created that you'd like to move.

5. In the Edit Bookmark window, tap **Bookmarks** or **Bookmarks Bar**, or whatever appears at the bottom of that window.

Continued . . .

Figure 2-7: From the Settings app, you can access settings for Safari.

The following security settings are enabled by default:

- **Accept Cookies**   Accepts cookies from websites you visit. Cookies are small text files that are stored on your iPad that tell a website what you prefer when visiting. Cookies can include your name, browsing history on the site, and information about items you've purchased.

- **Fraud Warning**   Warns you when you visit a fraudulent site that may try to get you to input personal information or information about your bank or credit cards. Some fraudulent websites also try to infect computers and devices with adware, spyware, and viruses.

- **Block Pop-ups**   Blocks pop-ups from websites that initiate them. Pop-ups are generally advertisements, and open in a new window.

QUICKSTEPS

**CREATING BOOKMARK FOLDERS
AND ADDING BOOKMARKS** *(Continued)*

6. Tap the folder you want to move the bookmark to.

7. Tap the appropriate "back" button to return to the Bookmarks list.

8. Tap **Done**.

TIP

You likely noticed the options to mail a link to this page, tweet, and print from the Add Bookmark icon in Safari. You can use these once you've configured Mail, set up a Twitter account, or acquired a compatible AirPrint printer to share specific webpages and information on them.

NOTE

Chapter 10 introduces all of the available settings in Safari. This section only discusses what you need to stay safe while online.

AutoFill is not enabled by default. When you enable AutoFill, you tell your iPad and Safari that you want it to populate web forms automatically. While this is a convenience, it can also create a security hole. If your iPad is stolen and is not protected by a passcode, the thief can access Safari and the forms can populate themselves.

You can change settings and preferences related to Safari for a better browsing experience from the Settings app on the Home screen. You can configure what search engine to use; whether or not to automatically fill in web forms with your name, address, and the like; and whether or not you want to show the Bookmarks Bar permanently in Safari. To access the settings:

1. Tap **Settings**.

2. Tap **Safari**.

3. Note the options in the right pane, and make changes as desired.

One thing you may want to configure in the Safari settings options is to always show the Bookmarks Bar. When enabled, the bookmarks you've saved to the Bookmarks Bar will appear below the current options and just above the webpage.

How to...

- Sync Your E-mail Accounts Using iTunes
- Add an Apple, Gmail, Yahoo!, or AOL Account
- Add Another Account Type
- Reading E-mail Messages on Multiple Devices
- Read E-mail
- Create a New E-mail
- Sending a Test E-mail
- Respond to E-mail
- E-mail Multiple Photos
- Use Gestures to Manage E-mail
- Sending Videos
- Open an Attachment
- Configuring Mail Settings
- Search for an E-mail
- Distinguishing Between Fetch and Push

Chapter 3

Communicating with Mail

The iPad comes with Mail, an e-mail management program already built in and ready to configure and use, available from the Home screen. With it you can easily view, receive, send, and reply to and forward e-mail; open many types of attachments; and even e-mail your own pictures to others.

Before you can use Mail, you have to tell Mail about your e-mail accounts. This requires you to provide your e-mail addresses and password, and possibly any associated settings, and that you test the e-mail accounts you configure to make sure they're working properly. Once you've done that, you're ready to use Mail.

NOTE

You can't send or receive e-mail unless you are connected to the Internet.

TIP

When instructed in this book to connect your iPad to your computer to sync it, remember you can connect physically using the supplied Universal Serial Bus (USB) cable, or you can sync over Wi-Fi if you've configured iTunes appropriately (and provided you plug your iPad in to an electrical outlet while it is connected to your local network). Of course, your computer must be turned on and accessible for syncing to occur as well.

Configure an E-mail Account

Your iPad comes with built-in support for e-mail accounts from Apple (iCloud and MobileMe), Gmail, Yahoo!, AOL, and Hotmail, as well as Microsoft Exchange accounts, typically used in larger enterprises. This means that setup is extremely easy for these types of accounts because Mail knows all of the required settings already and can configure them for you. You only need to know your user name and password to get started.

Mail also supports e-mail accounts from Internet service providers (ISPs) like Time Warner, Comcast, Verizon, and the like, although setting up these accounts sometimes takes a little more effort than the web-based e-mail services mentioned earlier. Whatever your situation, your first step in using Mail is to configure the accounts you want to use.

Sync Your E-mail Accounts Using iTunes

In this chapter, we outline how to set up your e-mail accounts manually using your iPad. However, if you're going to use the same e-mail accounts on your iPad that you already have configured on the computer you use to sync with it, you can sync the mail account settings using iTunes, and you won't have to input them manually as detailed here.

It's important to note that only the mail settings will be synced unless you say so otherwise from the other tabs in iTunes. Syncing e-mail settings won't sync your contacts, calendar events, and the like; that's an additional option. There's also no way to sync the folders or e-mail messages that are already on your computer in your e-mail program. When you opt to sync in this manner, you're only syncing the settings and nothing else.

To sync e-mail accounts using iTunes on a Windows-based PC (performing this task on a Mac is similar):

1. Connect your iPad to the computer you've been using to set up and sync your iPad. Make sure to connect to the computer you've been using since the beginning; do not connect your iPad to a different computer now, thinking that you'll just sync your mail accounts from it and nothing else; that won't work.

Figure 3-1: If you use the same e-mail accounts on your computer that you want to use on your iPad, you can sync the mail account settings from iTunes.

2. Wait while the initial syncing completes.

3. At your computer, in iTunes, select your iPad.

4. Click the **Info** tab.

5. Select **Sync Mail Accounts From**, and select the e-mail program you use from the list (see Figure 3-1).

6. Click **Apply**. Perform any additional tasks, including giving appropriate permissions.

7. When syncing completes, from your iPad, tap **Settings**.

8. Tap **Mail, Contacts, Calendars**.

9. Tap the mail account you just synced, and type your password (if prompted).

10. If applicable, choose what to sync.

11. Tap **Done**.

TIP

Mail is an option in iCloud settings, and can be enabled to keep iCloud mail in sync among multiple iDevices.

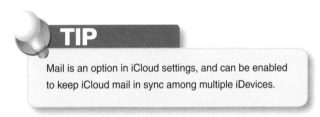
TIP

If you have a MobileMe account, follow instructions to migrate that account over to iCloud at http://www.apple.com/mobileme.

Add an Apple, Gmail, Yahoo!, or AOL Account

Some email accounts are simple to set up from your iPad. These are web-based accounts that your iPad already knows how to configure automatically. You may have a web-based account from Gmail or Hotmail (or others) already. Apple also offers their own web-based e-mail accounts. MobileMe is the older web-based account type from Apple, and iCloud is the newer one.

Web-based accounts are often preferable to other types of accounts (POP3, for instance) for use on tablets like the iPad because e-mail from these accounts is stored on Internet servers and is accessible from almost any Internet-enabled device. You can also store and organize e-mail in folders that you create on those sites, making it easier to manage the e-mail you want to keep on your iPad and other devices.

To configure a web-based e-mail account:

1. If you have not set up any e-mail accounts, on the Home screen, tap **Mail**. If you've already set up an e-mail account, tap **Settings** and then tap **Mail, Contacts, Calendars**.

Figure 3-2: Mail can configure various kinds of e-mail accounts automatically.

2. Tap the option that matches the type of account you want to configure (see Figure 3-2). If your web-based e-mail account isn't listed (Windows Live, for example), refer to the next section to configure that account (you'll have to tap **Other**).

3. Type the required information. You should only need to type your user name, e-mail address, password, and a description, shown in Figure 3-3.

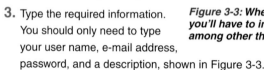

Figure 3-3: When creating an account manually, you'll have to input your user name and password, among other things.

4. Tap **Next**. Wait while the account settings are verified.

5. You may be prompted to configure additional settings, including whether or not to also download calendars, notes, and the like. Make choices as desired, and tap **Save**.

Add Another Account Type

If your e-mail account type isn't listed and you have to tap Other when setting up Mail, perhaps because you obtained your e-mail address from an Internet service you pay for, like Time Warner, Comcast, Verizon, or the like, you may have to provide some information manually. You'll be prompted for the information if it's required. If you don't know what to provide when prompted, call your Internet service provider for the details.

To create an e-mail account in Mail for a Post Office Protocol 3 (POP3) e-mail account:

1. If you're already in Mail and creating an account, tap **Other**. Otherwise:

   a. On the Home screen, tap **Settings**.

   b. Tap **Mail, Contacts, Calendars**.

   c. Tap **Add Account**.

   d. Tap **Other**.

TIP

If you're having trouble inputting the required information, try these typing tips:

- If you need to capitalize a letter, touch the **Up** arrow.

- If you need to locate an underscore, dash, or similar character, touch the **.?123** key. Note you may have to touch the **#+=** key to access additional characters.

TIP

If you need to configure a Microsoft Exchange account, ask your network administrator at work to help you.

2. Tap **Add Mail Account**.

3. Type your e-mail name, e-mail address, password, and description of the account.

4. Tap **Next**.

5. If prompted, type any required information for the server names, host names, user names, and so on. You can get this information from your e-mail provider. Tap **Save**. See Figure 3-4.

6. To edit the account, tap **Mail, Contacts, Calendars** and tap the account name. This is how you'll reenter information if you've encountered errors during the setup process.

Figure 3-4: Be careful when inputting information here; make sure it matches exactly the information you obtained from your ISP.

Work with E-mail

To read incoming mail and create your own, you first tap **Mail** to open it. If you've input more than one e-mail account, the first time you open Mail the Mailboxes page will appear and all of the accounts will be shown. (Subsequent visits to Mail will result in the app opening in the last view you used.) If this is the case, you can either tap a specific account to view only mail from that account, or you can tap **All Inboxes** to read all of your mail from all of your accounts in one window (see Figure 3-5).

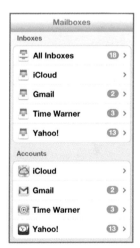

Figure 3-5: If you've configured more than one e-mail account, you'll have access to all of them in Mailboxes view.

READING E-MAIL MESSAGES ON MULTIPLE DEVICES

If you want to read your email on multiple devices, you may have to perform a few extra setup tasks.

THE PROBLEM

Some e-mail providers that are categorized as Other have their own e-mail servers in which to store e-mail until you retrieve it. Unlike web-based servers (AOL, Gmail, Hotmail, etc.), these providers will often delete e-mail after you've downloaded it once, generally to your computer at work or at home. E-mail providers do this to manage the data stored on their e-mail servers so they don't fill up with unwanted data.

THE RESULT

If your e-mail provider deletes e-mail from their servers after you've downloaded it at your computer, and if you get your e-mail at one of these computers before you can retrieve it on your iPad, the e-mail won't be available for download. It will have already been removed (or downloaded) from the server.

THE SOLUTION

Configure your home and/or work computer(s) to leave a copy of the messages on the server for a specified period. You'll need to open the e-mail program you use to get your mail and then search the Help files for something like "How to read e-mail messages on multiple computers." Once you know how to make the change, do so on every computer you get e-mail on.

Figure 3-6: When in any inbox or folder, a new option may appear allowing you to return to previous screens.

Read E-mail

To read all of your e-mail from every configured account (assuming you have multiple e-mail accounts configured):

1. Tap **Mail** on the Home screen.
2. Rotate the iPad so you are in landscape view. It's not required, but it makes using Mail easier.
3. If the Mailboxes page appears, under Inboxes, tap **All Inboxes**. (If you're in a specific Inbox, tap the appropriate "back" button first.)
4. Notice that a new button appears in the top-left part of the mail window: Mailboxes. You could tap **Mailboxes** to return to the previous screen (see Figure 3-6).
5. Tap any e-mail to read it, also shown in Figure 3-6.

To read e-mail from only one specific account:

1. If applicable, on the Home screen tap **Mail**.
2. If required, tap **Mailboxes** to return to the Mailboxes view.

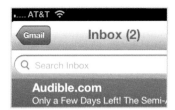

3. In Mailboxes, under Inboxes, tap any Inbox listed.

4. To return to the previous screen, tap the account name.

In Mailboxes view there's also an Accounts section. Tap an account name here to gain access to any account's Inbox, Drafts, Sent, and Trash folders, as well as other folders, if they exist. From this view you can review your sent items, access drafts (these are e-mails you've started and saved but have not sent), and even review what's

been deleted (in Trash). To return to previous tiers from inside these views, click the "back" button. The name of the button will change depending on where in the hierarchy you are.

When reading e-mail, you'll notice various arrows and buttons to help you navigate the interface, as well as options to enable you to perform tasks, such as delete an e-mail or reply to it. You'll see information across the top of the page to let you know you are connected to the Internet and options to access additional e-mail accounts. Figure 3-7 shows the icons that appear while reading an e-mail in landscape view.

TIP

Gmail and a few other web-based e-mail accounts will sync folders you've created at the website. This means you can create folders using your computer while, say, at the Gmail website, move data into them, and that information will be available from the Accounts section as shown in the illustration when you access it from your iPad.

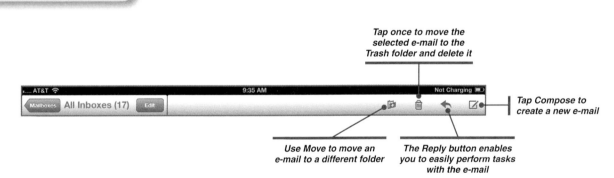

Figure 3-7: There are numerous icons in the Mail window when reading e-mail.

Create a New E-mail

To start a new e-mail, tap the **Compose** button. The Compose button is available in all Mail windows, even Mailboxes and an account's Trash folder. After tapping Compose, a new e-mail will open, along with the virtual keyboard, both shown in Figure 3-8.

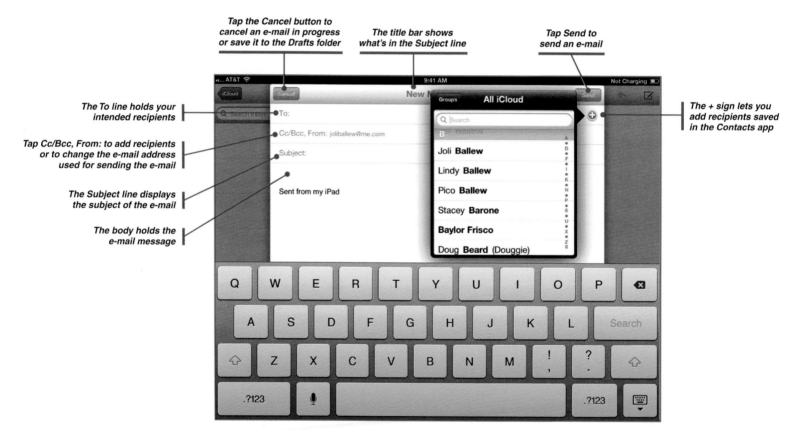

Tap the Cancel button to cancel an e-mail in progress or save it to the Drafts folder

The title bar shows what's in the Subject line

Tap Send to send an e-mail

The To line holds your intended recipients

Tap Cc/Bcc, From: to add recipients or to change the e-mail address used for sending the e-mail

The Subject line displays the subject of the e-mail

The body holds the e-mail message

The + sign lets you add recipients saved in the Contacts app

Figure 3-8: Tap Compose to open a new e-mail.

TIP

It's best to view Mail in landscape view for now. In landscape view you have easier access to all of the features. Portrait view does not offer the same amenities and can be more difficult to navigate.

QUICKSTEPS

SENDING A TEST E-MAIL

To test your Mail settings, on your iPad, compose and then send a test e-mail for each account you've configured. If you created an account for Gmail, send an e-mail from that account back to that account. And if you've also created an account for Time Warner, send an e-mail from the Time Warner account back to that account too. This will allow you to see if the e-mail accounts are properly configured, how long it takes to receive an e-mail in your Inbox once it's been sent, and that the e-mail also arrives on other e-mail–enabled devices you own.

TEST THE ACCOUNTS ON YOUR IPAD

To send a test e-mail:

1. Tap **Mail**.

2. Tap the **Compose** button.

3. Note the address in the From line. This is the account the message will be sent through. Type this address in the To line.

4. In the Subject line, type Test e-mail using my <account name> account.

Continued . . .

To compose a new e-mail:

1. Tap the **Compose** icon.

2. The To: line is active. Tap to type an e-mail address. Tap the plus sign (+) to add addresses from your contact list. If you tap the plus sign (+):

   a. Scroll or tap to locate the contact you want to add.

   b. Tap the contact name.

   c. If multiple e-mail accounts exist, tap the account you want to use.

3. To add addresses to the Cc: or Bcc: fields, tap the **Cc/Bcc, From:** line. Repeat step 2 to add e-mail addresses.

4. To change the account you want to send the e-mail from, tap the **Cc/Bcc, From:** line (if you did not tap it in step 3), tap the e-mail address shown, and tap a different account.

5. Tap the **Subject** line. Enter a subject.

6. Tap in the body. Enter body text.

7. Tap **Send**.

Respond to E-mail

As with other e-mail programs, you can reply to or forward e-mails you receive in Mail. To reply to or forward an e-mail:

1. Tap an e-mail you want to respond to or forward.

2. Click the **Reply**, **Reply All**, **Forward**, or **Print** button.

3. Tap **Reply, Reply All**, or **Forward**. (You'll only see Reply All if the e-mail was sent to multiple recipients.)

4. Complete the e-mail as desired, and tap **Send**.

| Reply |
| Reply All |
| Forward |
| Print |

E-mail Multiple Photos

You can e-mail a single photo or multiple photos using Mail. You do this from the Photos app, which you'll learn more about in Chapter 4. You can e-mail a single photo from any screen or view in Photos by tapping the **Share** button

QUICKSTEPS

SENDING A TEST E-MAIL *(Continued)*

5. Type <u>Test</u> in the body.

6. Repeat for each account you've configured. To change the account you're sending from, tap in the **Cc/Bcc, From** line, tap **From**, and tap a different account. (You may have to scroll to see all configured accounts.)

7. After sending all test e-mails, tap the **Refresh** button (located in the bottom-left corner next to Updated). Verify the e-mails arrived successfully for each account.

(the right-facing arrow) when it appears; but to send multiple photos, you must be in an album, in Photos, or in Photo Stream. To select multiple photos to e-mail:

1. Tap the **Home** button to access the Home screen.

2. Tap **Photos** and then tap **Albums**. (You could also select **Photos** or **Photo Stream**.)

3. Tap the album that contains the photos you want to send.

4. Tap the arrow in the top-right corner.

5. Tap each photo you want to send, up to three photos. Each time you tap a photo, a check mark will appear on it.

6. When your photos are selected, tap **Share** in the top-left corner, and then tap **Email**.

Continued . . .

SENDING A TEST E-MAIL *(Continued)*

TEST THE ACCOUNTS ON HOME AND WORK COMPUTERS

If you get mail from the same accounts you configured on your iPad on other devices, like home or work computers, iPhones, laptops, and the like, turn off your iPad and test those. From the other devices, perform the same e-mail test detailed earlier and wait for the e-mails you send to arrive back at those devices. Then, turn on your iPad, and verify that you can still receive those test e-mails after they've been downloaded to your other computers and mobile devices. If you do not receive them, refer to the "Reading E-mail Messages on Multiple Devices" QuickFacts earlier in this chapter to learn how to leave a copy of those e-mail messages on the server for each device you own. If you use an iCloud e-mail account, verify Mail is enabled by selecting **Settings I iCloud** on each of your iDevices.

TIP

Change the default signature "Sent from my iPad" to something more personal like your name, phone number, and other contact information. Select **Settings I Mail, Contacts, Calendars,** and then tap **Signature** to get started.

Use Gestures to Manage E-mail

It's easy to use gestures in Mail, if you know what they are! Perform these gestures and learn how to manage your e-mail with them:

- Tap the **Trash** icon to delete a message.
- In the left pane, flick left or right on any e-mail to access the Delete button. Tap **Delete** if desired.
- Tap **Edit**, tap to select the messages you want to delete, and then tap **Delete**.
- Tap the **Folder** icon to move a message to a different mailbox or folder. Next, navigate to the desired mailbox or folder. See Figure 3-9.

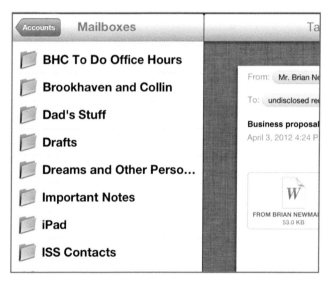

Figure 3-9: *If you have folders available you've created for a web-based e-mail account like Gmail, you can navigate there to save and organize e-mail you want to keep after you click the Move icon.*

QUICKSTEPS

SENDING VIDEOS

You can e-mail video as well as pictures. You may want to e-mail a short video you shot with the Camera app, for instance. Keep in mind when e-mailing video that it must be very short, because you can only attach so much data to an e-mail, and video files are quite large, and because e-mail providers often place limits on how large an attachment can be.

1. From the Home screen, tap **Photos**.

2. Locate the video you want to send. If you've taken a video with the Camera app, tap **Albums** and tap **Camera Roll**.

3. Tap the video.

4. Tap the **Share** button (the right-facing arrow).

5. Tap **Email Video**.

6. Complete the e-mail and send when ready.

NOTE

You can open a Microsoft Word document and read it, but you can't edit that document unless you have a compatible app, such as Apple's Pages. Similar limitations occur with other attachment types.

• Tap **Edit**, select the messages you want to move, and tap **Move**. You can also select **Delete** or **Mark**.

• **Pinch** your fingers outward to zoom in on a message; pinch inward to zoom out.

• **Double-tap** to zoom out on any zoomed-in message.

• Tap **Hide** or **Details** to see none or all recipients of a message, respectively.

• Tap a **contact's name** to add them to your Contacts list. Tap **Create New Contact** or **Add To Existing Contact** (see Figure 3-10).

• Tap the **blue dot** next to the subject line in the preview pane to mark a message as read; tap **Mark** at the end of the subject line of an e-mail to flag it or mark it as unread.

Open an Attachment

Attachments are add-ons to e-mails, and can be pictures, spreadsheets, videos, documents, or even presentations, among other things. You can open many

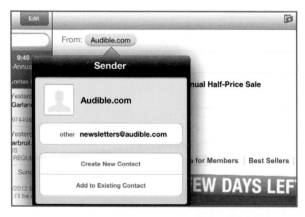

Figure 3-10: Add a contact to your Contacts list by tapping their name in an e-mail.

types of attachments on your iPad, although not quite as many as you can on a Mac or a PC. When there's an attachment, you'll see a paperclip icon.

You can open presentations, documents, and spreadsheets on your iPad by tapping the attachment icon that appears at the bottom of an e-mail. The attachment will open in a new window that enables you to scroll through the attachment, view it, and, if you have a compatible app, edit it. Table 3-1 outlines many of the compatible attachment types.

Pictures behave a little differently from other attached data. You don't have to open pictures separately or get an app—you already have one: Mail. Pictures will automatically appear in the body of an e-mail, and a momentary tap and hold on the image gives you the option to save the photo to the Photos app or copy it to paste it elsewhere.

FILE EXTENSION	FILE TYPE
.bmp	Bitmap
.doc	Microsoft Word
.docx	Microsoft Word
.htm	webpage
.html	webpage
.jpg	JPEG
.tiff	image
.gif	image
.key	Keynote
.numbers	Numbers
.pages	Pages
.pdf	Preview, Adobe Acrobat
.png	Portable Network Graphics
.ppt	Microsoft PowerPoint
.pptx	Microsoft PowerPoint
.rtf	Rich Text Format
.txt	text document
.vcf	contact information
.xls	Microsoft Excel
.xlsx	Microsoft Excel

Table 3-1: Some of the E-mail Attachments That Can Be Opened Using Mail

To try to view an attachment represented by a paperclip icon:

1. Tap **Mail** and tap the e-mail that contains the attachment.

2. Scroll to the bottom of the e-mail and tap the attachment icon.

3. To stop viewing the attachment (provided you were able to view it) if it's taking up the entire screen, tap at the top of the document, presentation, or spreadsheet; and then tap **Done**.

4. To save an image in an e-mail to your iPad, tap and hold briefly on the picture, and then tap one of the following options:

   a. **Save image**

   b. **Save # Images** (this option only appears if there are multiple images)

Search for an E-mail

Sometimes you need to locate an e-mail but can't remember where it is or who it was from, but you do remember what the e-mail was in reference to. In these cases, you can use the Search window to look through your e-mails, using a specific keyword. The more unique the word, the more likely you'll find what you're looking for; performing a search for a less unique word would result in a longer list of search results.

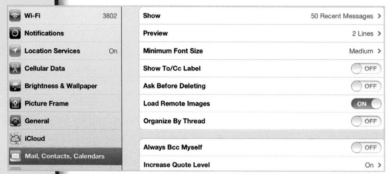

To search for a specific e-mail by keyword using Search:

1. Tap **Mail** and navigate to the account folder you want to search. You may want to select All Inboxes, a single Inbox, a Sent folder, or even an account's Trash folder.
2. Type a keyword into the Search window, above the list of e-mails in the left pane.
3. Review the results, noting you can sort by From, To, Subject, and All.
4. To open any result, tap it.

Personalize Mail

As you know, you can configure settings for Mail in the Settings app on the Home screen; that's where you go to create a second e-mail account. There are lots of other options to personalize Mail there. To see the options, tap **Settings** on the Home screen, and tap **Mail**, **Contacts**, **Calendars**.

QUICKSTEPS

CONFIGURING MAIL SETTINGS

To configure Mail settings, tap **Settings** on the Home screen, and tap **Mail, Contacts, Calendars**. Then follow the steps described in these sections.

SHOW MORE OR FEWER MESSAGES

1. Next to Show, tap how many messages are configured to show now.
2. Tap any other option.
3. Tap the "back" button for **Mail, Contacts, Calendar**.

SET A DEFAULT ACCOUNT

1. Tap the name next to Default Account.
2. Tap a different account.
3. Tap **Mail, Contacts, Calendar**.

CHANGE THE SIGNATURE

1. Tap **Signature**.
2. Type a new signature.
3. Tap **Mail, Contacts, Calendar**.

QUICKFACTS

DISTINGUISHING BETWEEN FETCH AND PUSH

In Settings, under Accounts, next to Fetch New Data is where you configure the Push or Fetch option. In order to understand which one to use, you need to understand their meanings.

PUSH

Push is a technology that allows Internet servers to send information to your iPad as soon as the message is

Continued . . .

DISTINGUISHING BETWEEN FETCH AND PUSH (Continued)

received by your e-mail provider on their servers. Some servers will push e-mail to you, but not all can do this. Supported e-mail providers include iCloud, Microsoft Exchange, and Yahoo!, but there are others. Be aware that using Push will require battery power and will minimize battery life. Transfers while connected via a cellular connection are counted toward your monthly data usage as well, so you might not want to enable Push if you are often on a cellular network and away from Wi-Fi. This can be a problem if you have a limited data plan.

FETCH

Many e-mail accounts aren't Push-compatible on the iPad. This means that no e-mail will arrive at your Inbox in Mail until you open Mail and access it. At that time, Mail will check for e-mail and obtain it from the e-mail servers. If this is inconvenient and you'd rather have Mail check for e-mail automatically, even when you aren't using it, you can configure your iPad to fetch your e-mail on a schedule, every 15, 30, or 60 minutes. You can also set Fetch settings to "Manually" so that no fetch occurs by default. As with Push, Fetch will cause your battery to drain more quickly. To maximize battery life, fetch less often or fetch manually. Fetch also kicks in for Push e-mail accounts if Push is turned off, so if you're watching your data usage, you may need to turn off Push and set Fetch to Manual.

To make a choice and configure settings in the Settings app:

1. Tap **Mail, Contacts, Calendars**.

2. Tap **Fetch** or **Push**, whatever is shown next to Fetch New Data.

3. Make your choices as desired.

Under Mail, and you'll have to scroll down to access this, you can configure various options for showing and previewing mail, including:

- **Show** to configure how many recent messages appear in your Inbox.

- **Preview** to configure how many lines are available in an e-mail preview, shown in the left pane while the iPad is in Landscape mode.

- **Minimum Font Size** to set how large or small text should appear in e-mails.

- **Show To/Cc Label** to show or hide the To/Cc label when composing a new e-mail.

- **Ask Before Deleting** to confirm or not confirm the deletion of e-mails.

- **Load Remote Images** to either load or not load images at the same time you load an e-mail. Turn off this feature if you're worried about cellular data usage.

- **Organize By Thread** to view e-mails by conversations instead of by the time an e-mail arrives.

- **Always Bcc Myself** to either always send a copy of the e-mail to yourself or not.

- **Increase Quote Level** to add a level of indentation when you forward or reply to a message.

- **Signature** to add and/or configure a signature for all outgoing e-mails. A signature appears at the bottom of the e-mail. By default, the included signature is "Sent from my iPad."

- **Default Account** to set which account will be used by default when sending photos from the Photo app and when launching e-mails from other apps.

You'll learn about the rest of the available settings in Chapter 10.

Chapter 4

Using the Camera, Displaying Photos, Viewing Videos, and Exploring FaceTime

Your iPad comes with two built-in cameras that you can use to take pictures and shoot videos, and there's a lens on the front and one on the back. The Photos app complements the camera, and enables you to view the photos and videos you've taken. You can also upload photos and videos from a camera or SD camera card (with an optional adapter), share photos in various ways, upload video to YouTube, and even print photos if you have a compatible printer, among other things. You can also use the video camera to have a video chat with another person who has a compatible device, using an app that's included, called FaceTime.

The Videos app is a related media app. It offers the ability to view videos you purchase, rent, or obtain, including movies, music videos, podcasts, iTunes U media, and other video data. While playing a video, you'll also have easy access to controls that enable you to pause, fast forward, and rewind the video.

In this chapter you'll learn about all of these things and more. You'll learn a little more about syncing too, because syncing all of the media you keep on your computer, purchase, or otherwise obtain can quickly fill up your iPad; you need to know how to sync only data you need to help manage what's on your iPad at any given time.

Use the Camera

You're probably anxious to take a picture, so we'll introduce that first. You take pictures using the Camera app, available from the default Home screen, provided you haven't moved it. The Camera app's screen is shown in Figure 4-1. There are only a few things to notice: the icon for the last picture taken, the Options button

Turn on the grid for the rear camera in still photo mode

Switch from photo mode to video mode

Options

View the last picture taken

Switch from the front- to rear-facing camera and vice versa

Figure 4-1: *There are only four items to become familiar with in the camera.*

(available when taking still pictures with the rear camera), the icon to switch from the back-facing lens to the front or vice versa, and the option to switch from photo mode to video mode (and back). Not shown here is the circular camera icon, located on the right side of the screen, in the middle. You'll see this shortly.

Take a Picture with the Camera

Taking a picture is very easy. Just tap the Camera icon on the Home screen to open the Camera app, choose which camera you want to use (front or rear), and tap the shutter button, located inside the Camera window, to snap your shot. The position of the shutter button has been moved in iOS5, and is now in the middle of the right side of the screen instead of on the bottom. You can also trigger the shutter using the volume up button on the outside of the iPad. It's important to practice this so you can do it quickly; you never know when the perfect shot is going to present itself!

1. If applicable, switch to the front- or rear-facing camera.
2. If applicable, tap the camera icon in the bottom-right corner to select the photo camera.
3. Aim, and if desired, tap the screen once to let the iPad adjust the exposure and focus.
4. Aim, and if desired, use a pinching motion to zoom in or out.
5. Aim again if you zoomed in or out, and then tap the camera icon in the middle of the right side of the screen to take the picture.
6. To view the picture in the Photos app, tap the thumbnail in the bottom-left corner. You'll learn more about the Photos app shortly.
7. If you viewed the picture in Step 6, tap the screen and tap **Done** when you're finished.

Take a Picture with Photo Booth

The Photo Booth app lets you apply effects to a subject and manipulate them prior to taking a picture. There are eight effects in total (nine if you count Normal as an effect), including but not limited to X-ray, Twirl, Thermal Camera, and Kaleidoscope. To use the Photo Booth app, you simply select the effect you like, use your finger to drag and manipulate the effect as desired, and snap

TIP

If you want to, tap anywhere on the screen to have the Camera app adjust the lighting balance and the focus on that particular area of the screen. When using the new iPad to photograph people, the camera uses face detection to automatically focus on and adjust the lighting balance on up to 10 faces. You can adjust the focus/lighting balance using a tap for the front or back camera while you are taking still photos or video.

TIP

If, while in the Photos app, you don't see Done, tap once on the photo. The controls disappear after a second or two of idle time.

NOTE

Tapping once on the screen to set the exposure and focus does not work with Photo Booth (as it did with the digital camera), and the zoom slider is not available either.

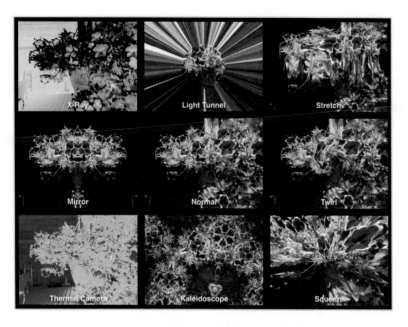

the picture. In Photo Booth, the icon you use to snap the picture is on the bottom, not on the right side where it is in the Camera app. Once you've taken a few photos, you can view them in full-screen mode and delete them easily, as well as e-mail and copy them.

1. Tap Photo Booth.
2. Tap the effect you like.
3. The Camera opens. In this window, drag your finger across the screen to apply additional effects. (This won't work if you chose Normal in Step 2.)
4. Tap the shutter icon (sometimes called the camera icon) to take the picture.
5. To return to Photo Booth to choose a different effect, tap the effect icon in the bottom-left corner; to switch camera lenses, tap the camera rotation icon in the bottom-right corner; to view the pictures you've taken, tap any thumbnail. These options and a few thumbnails are shown in Figure 4-2.

Figure 4-2: After you take a picture, you'll see additional options.

6. If you opt to tap a photo thumbnail in Step 5 (and you can tap the screen to make the controls reappear if they've gone missing), flick left and right to view the photos you've taken.

7. Tap the screen again to bring up the controls and thumbnails.

8. Tap any thumbnail and tap the **X** by it to delete it.

9. Tap any other thumbnail to view it. Tap the screen to make the controls reappear if they disappear.

10. To stop viewing photos and return to the Camera, tap the camera icon in the middle of the bottom of the screen.

11. To e-mail a photo you've taken:

    a. Tap any photo thumbnail if applicable.

    b. Tap the share button that appears in the bottom right of the screen when in thumbnail view.

    c. Tap any additional thumbnails to add photos.

    d. Tap **Email**. (Note you can also copy the photos to paste them somewhere else, or cancel the operation.)

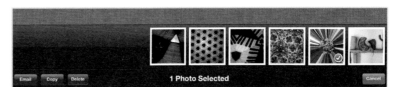

    e. Complete the e-mail as desired.

Take a Video

You may already know how to record video; it's intuitive, especially if you have already used the camera to take digital pictures. For the most part, you simply select the front- or rear-facing camera, make sure the slider is set to video mode, and tap the **Record** button that appears when the video camera is enabled. Tap the **Record** button again to stop recording. Figure 4-3 shows the options available when the video camera is selected.

TIP

There are multiple ways to get photos on to your iPad, including syncing with iTunes on a PC or Mac, getting them automatically from other iDevices via iCloud and Photo Stream, saving photos you get on your iPad in an e-mail, saving photos you find on the Internet (although this usually results in poor-quality photos), or using the optional Camera Connection Kit from Apple.

TIP

Don't see any photos? Read and work through the next section to copy photos to your iPad from your computer, or snap a few photos with the built-in camera.

TIP

While viewing any picture in full-screen mode, flick left or right to move among the photos in the album you're viewing.

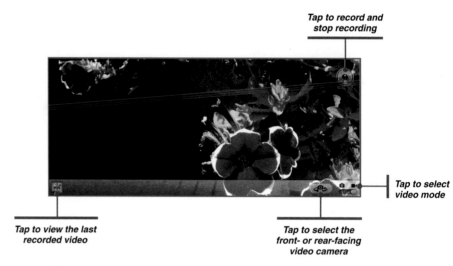

Tap to record and stop recording

Tap to select video mode

Tap to view the last recorded video

Tap to select the front- or rear-facing video camera

Figure 4-3: Recording is as simple as tapping the Record button.

As with taking digital pictures, a thumbnail appears after you've recorded some video. Tap it to view the recording (and share it) in the Photos app. Keep reading to learn more about the Photos app.

Explore the Photos App

The Photos app enables you to view and share photos with others easily. You can flick from left to right to change photos, flip the entire device to share a photo with someone sitting across from you, and tap and pinch to open an image in full-screen mode or zoom in on one. You can easily change views from portrait to landscape by simply turning the device 90 degrees left or right. You can even use your iPad as a digital photo frame and create your own slideshows of pictures with music!

To open the Photos app, just tap Photos on the Home screen. Photos will open, and you'll immediately notice tabs across the top of the page. What you see depends on the photos you've acquired on your iPad so far. You'll see some combination of Photos, Photo Stream, Albums, Events, Faces, and Places. And, you'll see Camera if you have a camera or camera card connected with the optional Camera Connection Kit. If it isn't already selected, tap Photos on the Home screen. If you've opened Photos before, tap the appropriate "back" buttons to return to the Photos main screen, shown in Figure 4-4.

Note what's available in the Photos interface. Specifically, note which of these tabs are available to you:

- **Photos** Use this tab to view thumbnails of all of your photos individually and to scroll through those thumbnails by flicking. Tap any photo to view it in full-screen mode.

- **Photo Stream** Use this tab to view photos you've taken and opted to sync with iCloud, using the Photo Stream feature. If you own multiple iDevices, what you see here will include photos you've taken with those devices (like an iPhone) that you've opted to save to iCloud. Figure 4-5 shows one place where you can enable Photo Stream on your iPad: Settings I iCloud I Photo Stream.

- **Albums** Use this tab to view your photos by albums. One album that is created by default is Camera Roll. If you purchase the optional Camera Connection Kit and upload photos using it, you'll see Last Import and All Imported as well. You'll see other folders too, because an album can also be something you create on your computer to organize your own photos (and sync), and you can create new albums on your iPad to organize the pictures you already have on it. When you sync the pictures you have in folders from your computer, you sync their respective folders to your iPad too.

- **Events** You will see an Events tab if you've somehow acquired photos on your iPad that the iPad can classify as an event, such as the date a particular group of photos were taken. This tab, if it isn't available now, will likely appear after you've imported photos using the optional Camera Connection Kit.

Figure 4-4: The tabs you see depend on the kind of data you have on your iPad.

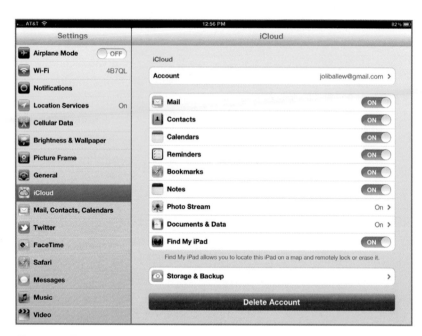

Figure 4-5: To enable Photo Stream, open the Settings app and configure iCloud settings.

- **Faces**   If you use a Mac and iPhoto or Aperture to organize and manage your photos using the built-in face-recognition feature, you'll see a Faces tab. If you don't use a Mac, you won't. Faces lets you mark a person's face with a name, and then the Photos app can sort photos by the person's name, based on the information about their face.

- **Places**   When you acquire photos on your iPad, they may be categorized into "Places" if the iPad can figure out where they were taken. If you've uploaded or synced photos taken with a GPS-enabled camera or iPhone, you may see results in the Places tab, as shown in the following illustration.

- **Camera**   Use this tab to select what photos to import when the Camera Connection Kit is connected.

Email Photo

Assign to Contact

Use as Wallpaper

Tweet

Print

Copy Photo

Figure 4-6: There are many ways to share a photo from the Photos app, including tweeting it.

NOTE

You'll see the Trash icon only if you took the picture with the iPad, have it stored in Photo Stream, or if it's an iPad screen capture.

You can tap any photo from any of these tabs to view it in full-screen mode. You'll see additional options when you view a photo. To view any photo and the additional options, tap it. The additional options will appear at the top of the page. You can use the Share icon (a right-facing arrow) to share the photo with others via e-mail or Twitter, or to assign it to a contact or as wallpaper, among other things. You can also print and copy the photo. Figure 4-6 shows these options and the others that appear across the top of a photo when it's in full-screen mode.

Upload Photos from an SD Card or Camera

There are several ways to copy (upload) pictures from your camera or camera phone to your iPad. You can sync pictures using your computer, e-mail them to yourself, or connect the optional SD Camera Connection Kit or SD card reader and upload them using Photos, among other things. The latter is the easiest if you have compatible hardware.

If you've purchased the Camera Connection Kit, to upload pictures currently on an SD card or on the camera itself:

1. Connect the appropriate Camera Connection Kit adapter to the iPad via the 30-pin port at the bottom.

2. Then do one of the following:

   a. Turn on your digital camera and position any settings for playback on that camera, as warranted, and connect the camera to the adapter using the camera's Universal Serial Bus (USB) cable.

   b. Insert the camera's SD card into the adapter.

3. Tap the **Home** key to wake the iPad, if necessary.

4. Wait while the pictures are read.

5. If you tap **Import All**, all photos will be copied to your iPad. If you want only a subset, tap the pictures you'd like to import, and then tap **Import**. From there tap **Import All** or **Import Selected**.

6. When the import process has completed, either tap **Delete** to delete the imported media from the camera or **Keep** to keep it.

Use Touch Techniques to View Photos

When you tap a thumbnail of a photo, it appears in full-screen mode. Figure 4-7 shows this screen. The icons will disappear in three or four seconds if you don't use them. You can tap once on the photo to bring them back. Thumbnails of the other photos in the album you're viewing appear across the bottom (not shown), and you can tap any thumbnail or slide your finger across them to skip to another photo quickly.

You can use various touch techniques to view photos, including using a tap, flick, or pinch and physically repositioning the iPad. To view photos using touch techniques:

- **Tap a thumbnail** to view the photo in full-screen mode.
- **Tap a picture** in full-screen mode to view the controls. Tap again to hide these controls.
- **Pinch with two fingers** to zoom in on a photo or to open any folder of photos.
- **Flick** right to left, left to right, top to bottom, or bottom to top to move around in a screen that is longer than one page or to move from photo to photo when viewing pictures in full-screen mode. You can also flick if you've zoomed in on a photo.
- **Double-tap** to zoom in on and then zoom out of a photo.
- **Pinch with five fingers** to close the Photos app.
- **Drag four fingers upward** to show the multitasking bar (do the opposite to hide it).

This offers information about the placement of the photo in the folder

Open the editing options including Rotate, Enhance, Red-Eye, and Crop

Configure slideshow options and start a slideshow

The "back" button becomes available when you view a photo in full-screen mode

Delete the photo

Share a photo via e-mail, message, tweet, or print; to copy the image to paste it elsewhere; or assign to a contact or use as wallpaper

Figure 4-7: When viewing a photo, tap once to see the controls shown here (you won't see all controls in all instances).

CREATING AND VIEWING A SLIDESHOW

There are two ways to enjoy a slideshow of photos. You can create and view a slideshow in the Photos app when your iPad is unlocked, or you can view a slideshow with Picture Frame while your iPad is locked. Picture Frame is an option from the Lock screen, allowing you to offer a slideshow without opening up access to your iPad. The icon looks like a flower.

CREATE A SLIDESHOW

To create a slideshow in the Photos app:

1. Tap **Photos**, tap **Albums** (you may have to tap a "back" button before you can access Albums), and tap an album you'd like to display in a slideshow. Alternately, tap the **Photos** tab to use all of your photos.

2. Tap **Slideshow**.

3. To play music with your slideshow:

   a. Move the Play Music slider to On.

   b. Tap **Music** and tap a song.

4. Tap **Transitions** and tap a transition.

5. Tap **Start Slideshow**.

You can change how long to play each slide and/or to repeat or shuffle photos from the Home screen. Tap **Settings**, tap **Photos**, and make your changes as desired.

Continued...

Copy a Photo

There are many reasons why you would want to copy a photo, but you'll probably want to paste it into the body of an e-mail or a compatible app. You may have apps that allow you to paste into them, such as iWork apps like Pages, Numbers, and Keynote.

To copy a photo:

1. In Photos, locate the picture you want to copy.

2. Tap the photo to view it in full-screen mode.

3. Tap and hold on the screen for a second or two, and tap **Copy** when it appears.

4. Open an app that supports the Paste command and can accept photos (Notes can't). For example, you can open a new Mail message.

5. Tap and hold, and tap **Paste** when applicable.

Edit a Photo

Sometimes, a photo needs a little touching up. It may need to be rotated, enhanced, cropped, or you may need to remove red eye. You can do this from the Edit option when a photo is in full-screen mode.

To get started, locate a photo that needs editing and tap it. In full-screen mode, tap **Edit**. Note the options at the bottom of the page:

- **Rotate** When you tap Rotate, the picture is rotated 90 degrees counterclockwise. You can tap multiple times.

- **Enhance** When you tap Enhance, automatic enhancements are applied. You can save or undo the changes.

QUICKSTEPS

CREATING AND VIEWING A SLIDESHOW (Continued)

USE PICTURE FRAME

To configure settings for Picture Frame, tap **Settings** and tap **Picture Frame**. Choose a transition, opt to zoom in on faces, or shuffle the pictures, as desired. You can also opt to show all photos, only albums, or only events. Default settings are configured if you do not want to make changes. With that done, to start or stop Picture Frame:

1. Press the **Sleep/Wake** button to lock the iPad.

2. Press the **Sleep/Wake** button again or the **Home** button to view the lock screen.

3. Tap the **Picture Frame** icon next to the slider to start the show.

4. Tap anywhere on the iPad to access the Lock Screen again, where you can tap the **Picture Frame** icon to stop the show.

Figure 4-8: Cropping lets you remove unwanted parts of a photo.

TIP

You can show any slideshow (or any photo or album) that's on your iPad on an Apple TV if you're connected to your home network via Wi-Fi and if the required hardware is available on that network. This works automatically through your Wi-Fi network, with no setup needed. Tap the **AirPlay** icon to start the show. Alternately, you can physically connect to your high-definition TV (HDTV) using the Apple Digital AV Adapter to share a slideshow.

- **Red-Eye**   When you tap Red-Eye, you are prompted to tap once on each eye that is red. You can tap again to undo this if you tap in the wrong place.

- **Crop**   When you tap Crop, a grid appears. Drag from the corners and sides to crop as desired, and then tap Crop. See Figure 4-8.

Print a Photo

To print from the Photos app, you must have a compatible AirPrint printer available. AirPrint works with other apps too, including Safari, Mail, iWork, PDFs in iBooks, and more. To print from Photos, tap the **Share** icon, and tap **Print**.

Explore Photo Stream

Photo Stream, in conjunction with iCloud technology, lets you take photos on one iDevice (like an iPad) and have them automatically appear on the others (like an iPhone or iPod touch). Photo Stream photos also appear in iPhoto on a Mac, if you have one. You don't have to sync an iDevice to your computer and then to other devices, and you don't have to send the photos via e-mail; when Photo Stream is enabled, photos simply appear.

Photo Stream only holds your latest 1,000 photos. This guarantees you won't run out of storage space in iCloud. If you want to edit a photo or save it permanently on any iDevice, you'll have to save the photo to the Camera Roll album in the Photos app. This will keep it from "rolling off" your iDevice if you amass more than 1,000 photos there. You'll learn how to do this shortly.

Photos stored with Photo Stream in iCloud are stored for 30 days. During those 30 days, you need to sync your iPad to your computer. When you do, all of your Photo Stream photos will be synced there, so you will never lose them. This means that even if you amass more than 1,000 and they disappear from your iDevices, they'll still appear on your computer.

If you want to enable Photo Stream, you can do it in several ways. One is to open Settings and tap Photos. From there you can enable Photo Stream on your iPad. Once enabled, open the Photos app and touch the Photo Stream tab.

The first time you open Photo Stream while connected to a Wi-Fi network, you may see photos begin to appear as they are synced. Photos may appear somewhat slowly; but never mind that—they'll get synced eventually. Newly synced photos will appear at the bottom of the Photo Stream list of photos.

Once photos appear in the Photos app under the Photo Stream tab, look to see if there are any you'd like to save to your iPad. If so:

1. Tap the **Share** button.
2. Tap the photos you want to save. Checkmarks will appear on the photos you select.

TIP

When you make changes with any editing tool, you'll have to tap Save to apply those changes to the Camera Roll album. Revert To Original is also an option. Note that the edited version replaces the original version when you tap Save.

TIP

The photos you edit are stored in the Camera Roll album of the Photos app.

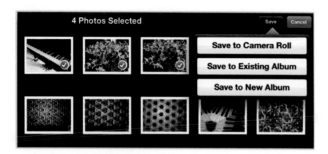

3. Tap **Save**.

4. Tap:

   a. **Save To Camera Roll** to save the photos to the Camera Roll album in the Photos app.

   b. **Save To Existing Album** to name the album you want to save to.

   c. **Save To New Album** to create a new album, name it, and save the photos there.

5. You'll be prompted to complete one more step if you choose to save the photos to an album. You'll either need to choose the album you want to save to or type a name for a new album you want to create.

To create an album from your iPad, open any album that already contains photos, click the **Share** button, and click **Add To New Album**. Follow the prompts to create the new album. You can then choose that album later to save additional pictures to it.

Explore the Videos App

The Videos app is where you watch music videos, movies, and TV shows you purchase or rent from iTunes, and movies you've synced from your computer. You can also watch video you've downloaded from iTunes U, video podcasts, and other kinds of media. The Videos app supports high-definition and standard-definition videos and movies, supports closed captioning, and can be viewed in widescreen mode, among other things. Most of the tabs in the Videos app, like the tabs in the Photos app, only appear if you have related types of media.

You will see at least some of these tabs in the Videos app, shown in Figure 4-9:

- **Store**   Offers access to the iTunes Store, where you can obtain video media.

- **Movies**   Holds movies you've purchased or rented.

- **TV Shows**   Holds TV shows you've acquired. You won't see this tab if you don't have any TV shows.

- **Podcasts**   Holds video podcasts you've acquired. You won't see this tab if you haven't downloaded any video podcasts.

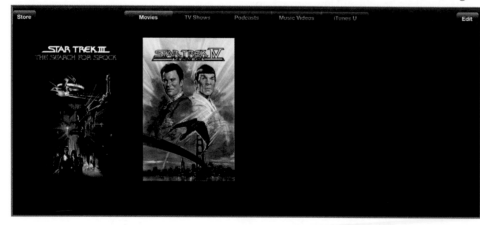

Figure 4-9: The Videos app offers tabs where you access related media.

USING PHOTOS FOR CONTACTS AND WALLPAPER

Any picture on your iPad can be assigned to a contact or used as wallpaper. Contacts are detailed in Chapter 8, and hold information about people you communicate with. Wallpaper is the picture you see when your iPad is locked, as well as the picture you see on any Home screen.

ASSIGN A PHOTO TO A CONTACT

To assign a photo to a contact:

1. Tap **Photos**.
2. Tap the photo you want to use.
3. Tap the **Share** button.
4. Tap **Assign To Contact**.
5. Tap the desired contact.
6. If desired, move and scale the image by dragging your finger on it.
7. Tap **Use**.

SET A PHOTO AS WALLPAPER

To set a photo as wallpaper:

1. Tap **Photos**.
2. Tap the photo you want to use.
3. Tap the **Share** button.
4. Tap **Use As Wallpaper**.
5. Tap **Set Lock Screen**, **Set Home Screen**, or **Set Both**.

Edit   Slideshow

- **Email Photo**
- **Assign to Contact**
- **Use as Wallpaper**
- **Tweet**
- **Print**
- **Copy Photo**

- **Music Videos** Holds music videos you've purchased from iTunes. You won't see this tab if you don't have any music videos.

- **iTunes U** Holds media obtained from iTunes U. You won't see this tab if you don't have any iTunes U media.

Play a Movie

You need to have movies or videos on your iPad to view them. You can obtain video media by syncing it from your computer; you can rent or purchase movies from iTunes; and you can download free podcasts from various places, including iTunes, which is detailed in Chapter 6.

You can also play movies that are in your iCloud storage if you have paid for Apple's Music Match service. In this case, if the movie is in iCloud, an iCloud icon will show under the thumbnail. When you click to play a video from the iCloud, there will be a slight delay while downloading and buffering begins. Eventually, the video will be downloaded onto your iPad, and you'll be able to watch it even when you have no Internet connection.

To find and play a video using the Videos app:

1. Tap the Videos app on the Home screen.
2. Tap the tab that contains the media you want to view.
3. Tap any video to see more information.
4. Tap **Play**.

Movies   Info   Chapters

Star Trek IV: The Voyage...
PG, Paramount Pictures, 2001

Summary

It's the 23rd century, and a mysterious alien power is threatening Earth by evaporating the oceans and destroying the atmosphere. In a frantic attempt to save mankind, Kirk and his crew must time travel back to 1986 San Francisco where they find a world of punk, pizza and exact-change buses that are as alien as anything they've ever encountered in the far reaches of the galaxy. A thrilling, action-packed Star Trek adventure!

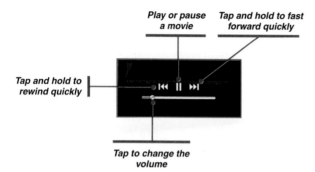

Play or pause
a movie

Tap and hold to fast
forward quickly

Tap and hold to
rewind quickly

Tap to change the
volume

Figure 4-10: Easily control
the playback of a movie.

TIP

If you have an Apple TV installed on your home network, you'll also see an AirPlay icon in addition to the available controls.

NOTE

If you record video with a digital camera and upload that video to your iPad with the optional Camera Connection Kit or media card reader, iPad-compatible videos will appear in the Photos app, not the Videos app. The same holds true of video you take with your iPad's video camera.

Use Video Controls

When watching a movie, you'll have controls available to you. To use the video controls while watching a movie:

1. Tap the screen.

2. Tap any control to apply it (see Figures 4-10 and 4-11).

3. Tap the screen to hide the controls. They will disappear automatically after about six seconds. Tap again to make those controls reappear.

Sync Only Specific Photos or Videos

You learned a little about syncing in Chapter 1, and you'll learn even more in Chapter 9. However, it's important to address syncing media here as well, because media takes up lots of storage space and can easily fill your iPad with data. The best way to handle this storage issue is to regularly review the movies, TV shows, and other media that are stored on your iPad. You should make sure to regularly remove movies and other media you've seen and only keep video media you haven't seen or plan to watch again soon on your iPad.

If you acquired your media from somewhere other than the iTunes Store, sync your media to your computer before you delete it from your iPad. If you've purchased videos from the iTunes Store, you don't have to do that. You can

Use the scrubber bar
to move through a
video quickly

Denotes how
much time is left
in the video

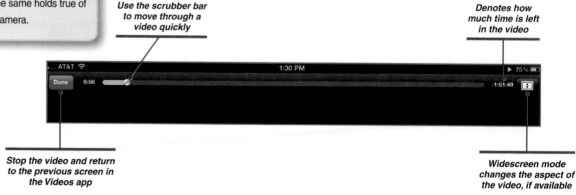

Stop the video and return
to the previous screen in
the Videos app

Widescreen mode
changes the aspect of
the video, if available

Figure 4-11: These controls help you navigate the movie.

View: Movies   All   Not On This iPad

Q Search   Sort by: Most Recent

Star Trek II: The Wrath of Khan
Sci-Fi & Fantasy
1.59 GB

Star Trek III: The Search for S...
Sci-Fi & Fantasy
1.50 GB

Star Trek IV: The Voyage Home
Sci-Fi & Fantasy
1.74 GB

redownload your purchases if you want to put them back on your iPad. (Make sure you're connected to a Wi-Fi network if you do.)

To sync with your computer and iTunes:

1. Connect your iPad to your computer with the USB cable.

2. In iTunes, in the left pane, click your iPad.

3. In iTunes, click **Movies**.

4. Click **Sync Movies**.

5. Deselect, if applicable, **Automatically Include**.

6. Select only the media you want to sync.

7. Repeat with other applicable categories, such as TV Shows, iTunes U, or others.

8. Click **Apply**.

Note that there are additional options in iTunes. You can select Automatically Include, for instance, and select an option such as All Unwatched, 5 Most Recent, and other options. You can deselect this option and choose to sync media you've purchased on your computer or your iPad.

Explore FaceTime

FaceTime is an app that lets you hold video chats with others. People you want to video-chat with must have an iPad, iPhone, iPod touch, or a Mac; the devices must run iOS5 or later; and the devices must be connected to Wi-Fi. (A Mac can be connected via Ethernet and it must be running Mac OS X 10.6.6 with all available security updates installed.) The other people must have FaceTime set up as well. They have to provide an Apple ID and password, and provide or verify the e-mail address they want to associate with it.

TIP

If you want to "stream" a movie that's playing on your iPad to your television and watch it there (and control it from your iPad), tap the **AirPlay** icon next to the fast-forward button in the controls. You'll see the icon you need to tap to connect if you're connected to your home network via Wi-Fi and if you have an Apple TV installed on your network.

NOTE

If you buy a movie or TV show, it's yours (unlike renting). The next time you open the Videos app on your iPad, it'll still be there.

TIP

Tap **Settings** and tap **FaceTime** to change or add an e-mail address, or to turn FaceTime on or off.

Because calls are placed by tapping a contact's e-mail address, when you first tap FaceTime, you'll be prompted to provide your own Apple ID and password and then tell FaceTime what e-mail address you want to use when people call you. With that done, FaceTime is ready to use.

Info   Edit

na Reynolds
ffice Girl

76-0807

areynolds@gmai...

How to...

Chapter 5
Getting and Listening to Music and Audio

The Music icon is positioned at the bottom of your iPad on the Dock (unless you've moved it), and when touched, allows you to access the music on your iPad, play it, and view album art and track information, among other things. While playing music, you'll have access to familiar controls, like pause, skip, and repeat, and some that you may not be so familiar with, like shuffle and Genius. You can use the Music app to create playlists, sort your music, and search for specific music by its attributes too. The Music app can easily run in the background while you do other things on your iPad. You can even use the volume controls on the outside of your iPad when your iPad is locked and the screen is dark.

Obtain Music

If you haven't synced any music (or other audio media) to your iPad yet, it's time! There are a few ways to do this, and you'll probably apply a combination of these techniques to populate your iPad with music and media. Here are the most common copy options:

- You can physically connect your iPad to your computer and configure iTunes to sync the desired music. Once configured, the sync will take place automatically each time you connect your iPad to your computer in the future. This is detailed in the next section.

- You can configure iTunes to sync music to your iPad over your Wi-Fi network. You must enable this in iTunes on your computer from the Summary tab. Wi-Fi sync requires your computer to be connected to the same Wi-Fi network, and iTunes must be running on your computer. The iPad must be plugged in to a wall outlet, too. Sync will occur once a day, when all conditions are met. You can force a sync from your iPad (select **Settings I General I iTunes Wi-Fi Sync**); again, however, all conditions must be met for the Sync Now option to be available.

- You can purchase music from iTunes, either on your iPad or on your computer. New purchases should be automatically downloaded to the device from which you purchased it. (You can set up other authorized computers and iOS devices to automatically download purchases made on other devices.) You can tailor which purchases are downloaded to the iPad and only automatically download just music, just apps, just books, or a combination of these.

- You can download music you've already purchased from the iTunes Store directly to your iPad from the iTunes Store's Purchased tab. See Figure 5-1.

Sync Personal Music Files

You may have a music collection on your computer that you'd like to also have on your iPad. To copy music that is on your computer to your iPad, you must set up syncing. Once syncing is set up, any changes made to either music library (on the iPad or the computer) are automatically synced each time you connect the two devices. It is best to put all of your music on one computer (the computer you used to activate your iPad) and use that computer to copy, manage, and sync music between the two.

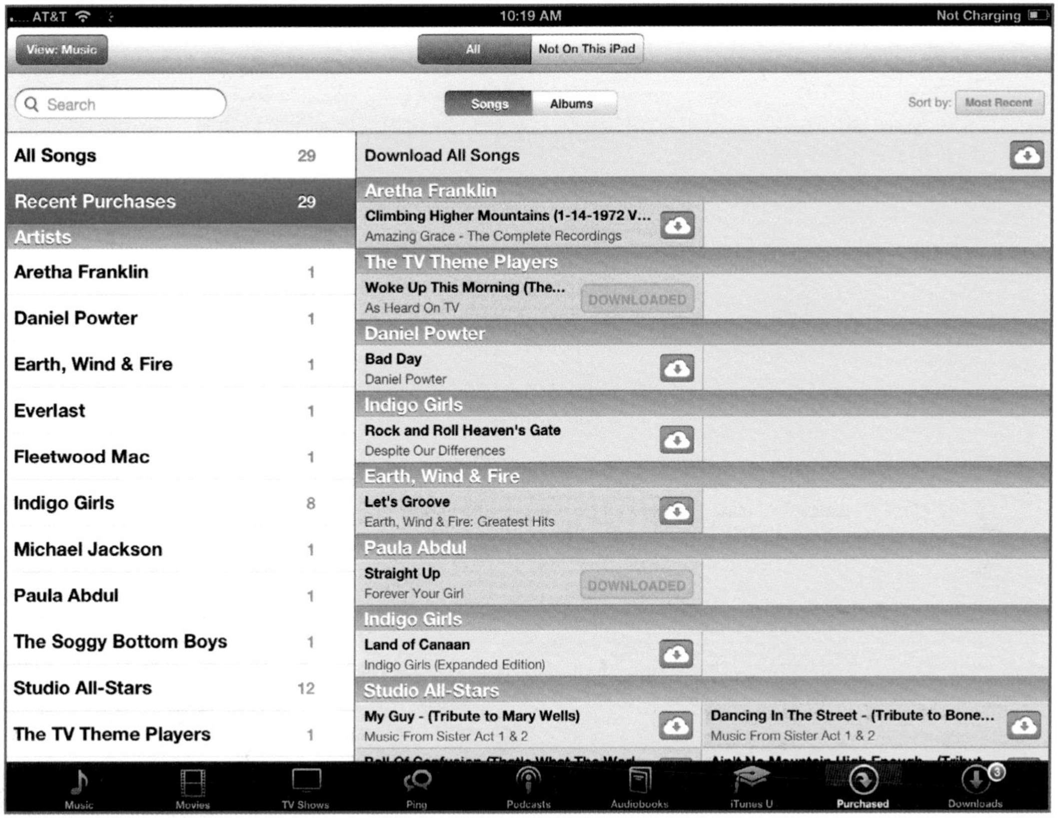

Figure 5-1: A cloud icon means the item is available to download on your device.

To sync music from your PC to your iPad using iTunes (performing this on a Mac is similar):

1. Connect your iPad physically or via Wi-Fi to your computer.

2. In the source pane in iTunes, on your computer, click the icon for your iPad.

3. Click the **Music** tab. See Figure 5-2.

4. Select the desired syncing options. (If you paid for iTunes Match, you won't see what's shown in Figure 5-2.)

5. If desired, select **Automatically Fill Free Space With Songs**.

6. Click **Sync** (not shown).

TIP

Remember that you can sync without physically connecting your iPad to your computer, provided your iPad is plugged into a wall outlet and is connected to your home network, and that the computer is awake, iTunes is open, and Wi-Fi syncing is enabled in iTunes.

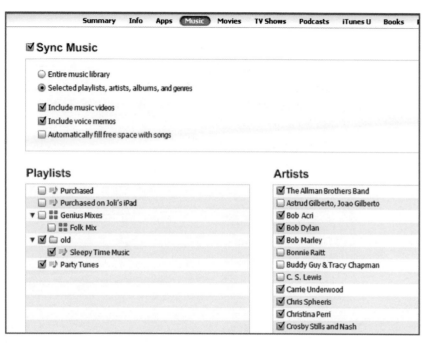

Figure 5-2: In iTunes, on your computer, and with your iPad connected, click the Music tab to see your syncing options.

Sync Audiobooks

You can get audiobooks from the iTunes Store, detailed in Chapter 6. If you have an audiobook already, either one you've purchased or one you've synced from your computer, you can find it and listen to it using the Music app on the iPad. For more information on purchasing and downloading audiobooks from iTunes, refer to that chapter. Your iPad also supports Audible files, and Audible is one of the largest audiobook companies in the world. In addition to audiobooks, Audible.com offers radio shows, podcasts, stand-up comedy, and speeches from people who shape culture, politics, and business.

If you have audiobooks, you can sync them in the same manner as you sync music. Once connected, select your iPad in the source pane of iTunes, click the **Books** tab, and opt to sync all of your audiobooks or select specific books to sync. (If you have a lot of digital books, you'll need to scroll to the bottom of the page to see your audiobooks.)

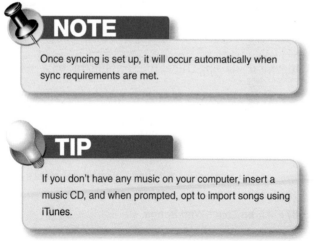

NOTE

Once syncing is set up, it will occur automatically when sync requirements are met.

TIP

If you don't have any music on your computer, insert a music CD, and when prompted, opt to import songs using iTunes.

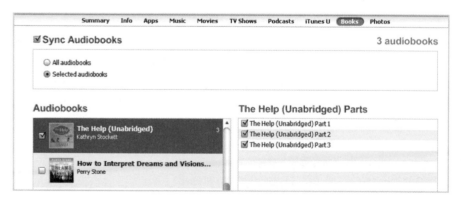

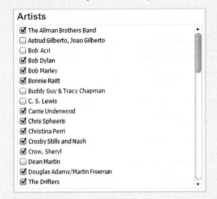

SYNCING ONLY MUSIC FROM SPECIFIC ARTISTS

There are many options for syncing music, and one is to choose only a specific artist or artists.

1. Connect your iPad to the computer you sync it with, either wired or wirelessly.

2. Select your iPad in the source pane.

3. Click the **Music** tab.

4. Click **Selected Playlists, Artists, Albums And Genres**.

5. Scroll down to **Artists**.

6. Select the artists you want to sync.

Artists

- ☑ The Allman Brothers Band
- ☐ Astrud Gilberto, Joao Gilberto
- ☐ Bob Acri
- ☑ Bob Dylan
- ☑ Bob Marley
- ☑ Bonnie Raitt
- ☐ Buddy Guy & Tracy Chapman
- ☐ C. S. Lewis
- ☑ Carrie Underwood
- ☑ Chris Spheeris
- ☑ Christina Perri
- ☑ Crosby Stills and Nash
- ☑ Crow, Sheryl
- ☐ Dean Martin
- ☑ Douglas Adams/Martin Freeman
- ☑ The Drifters

7. Continue selecting items from Playlists, Genres, and Albums as desired.

8. Click **Apply**.

NOTE

You can also opt to sync specific genres, albums, and playlists.

Sync Podcasts

Podcasts are digital media files, similar to audiobooks, that are released to the public and often downloaded through web syndication. They aren't live, although some are recorded live and uploaded later. After you've downloaded an audio podcast, it will appear in Music, in the Podcasts section from the More tab. This is shown in the first illustration. You won't see Podcasts in the More list if you don't have any. Video podcasts will appear under the Podcasts tab of the Videos tab, shown in the second illustration. Again, you won't see the Podcasts tab in the Videos app if you don't have any video podcasts.

Browse Music

To play music on your iPad, you open the Music app, browse for the media you want to play, and tap it to play it. You can browse for media in many ways:

TIP

You can find a long list of podcasts at a podcast directory site such as www.podcastdirectory.com.

NOTE

If you can't find the media you're looking for in the Music app, tap **More**.

by playlists, songs, artists, albums, genres, and composers, or you can search for something by typing a song name, artist name or other metadata. Depending on the media you've synced or acquired, you may also be able to browse categories including Podcasts, Audiobooks, and by music that's been shared on your network. (If you signed up for iTunes Match, you'll see cloud icons in various lists.)

Here are the categories you'll see across the bottom of the Music app:

- **Store**   This tab offers access to the iTunes Store, where you can buy music and other media.
- **Playlists**   This tab offers access to playlists you've synced or created. You'll learn more about playlists later in this chapter. For now, it's enough to know that a playlist is a group of songs.
- **Songs**   This tab offers access to all of your songs, listed alphabetically. You can flick to scroll through them quickly. You can also tap in the Search window to search for a song by its title. Figure 5-3 shows this.
- **Artists**   Click to view your music by artist. If you have multiple albums by the same artist, tap the artist's name to view the albums.

Galileo	Indigo Girls	Rites of Passage	4:14
Ghost	Indigo Girls	Retrospective	5:16
Gold Dust Woman	Fleetwood Mac	Rumours	5:03
Graceland	Paul Simon	Graceland	4:51
Hammer and a Nail	Indigo Girls	Nomads Indians Saints	3:51
Jar of Hearts	Christina Perri	Jar of Hearts - Single	4:08
Jesus, Take The Wheel	Carrie Underwood	Jesus, Take the Wheel - Single	3:01
Jonas & Ezekial	Indigo Girls	Rites of Passage	4:09
The Lion, Witch, Wardrobe 01	C. S. Lewis	Narnia 2 - The Lion, the Witch, and the War...	1:09

Store	Playlists	Songs	Artists	Albums	More	

*Figure 5-3: **All of your songs are available from the Songs tab, and a Search window is available at the bottom of the screen.***

- **Albums**   Click to view your albums in alphabetical order. If you know what album you want to listen to, this is the best way to find it.

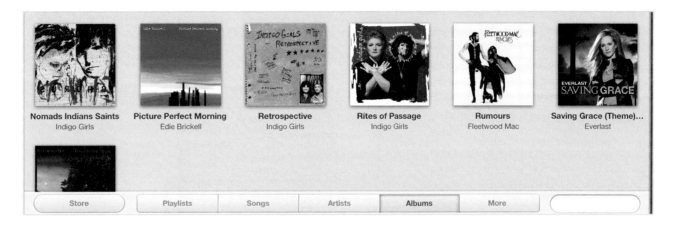

Nomads Indians Saints
Indigo Girls

Picture Perfect Morning
Edie Brickell

Retrospective
Indigo Girls

Rites of Passage
Indigo Girls

Rumours
Fleetwood Mac

Saving Grace (Theme)...
Everlast

| Store | Playlists | Songs | Artists | Albums | More | |

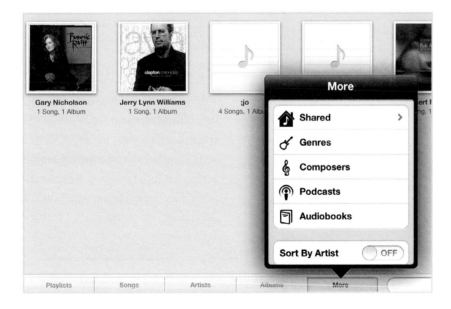

Gary Nicholson
1 Song, 1 Album

Jerry Lynn Williams
1 Song, 1 Album

:jo
4 Songs, 1 Albu

More

🏠 Shared   >

🎸 Genres

🎼 Composers

📡 Podcasts

📖 Audiobooks

Sort By Artist   ○ OFF

| Playlists | Songs | Artists | Albums | More | |

- **More**   Click to access additional categories, including Genres and Composers, and specialty categories, including Audiobooks and Podcasts.

- **Genres**   iTunes classifies your music automatically by genre. Genres can include Folk, Rock, Alternative, and Soundtrack, among others. If you know you want to listen to a specific genre (say Folk, when your mom stops by), this is the place to go.

- **Composers**   Click to view your music by composer. The composer of a song is not always the artist who sings it.

- **Podcasts**   This library only holds media deemed by the Music app to be podcasts.

- **Audiobooks**   This library only holds media deemed by the Music app to be audiobooks.

SEARCHING FOR A SONG

If your music library is large, you may want to search for a specific song instead of scrolling through the Songs list. You can search for media from the Search window.

1. From the Home screen, tap **Music** to open the Music app.

2. Tap inside the Search window.

3. Type the first few letters of the title of the song. (You can also search by album or artist name.)

4. Tap the desired result to play the song.

Play Media and Use Media Controls

Playing a song is one of the simplest things you can do with the Music app. You tap it. Once a song is playing, there are a few things you'll want to do right away, including changing the volume.

To adjust the volume:

- Locate the volume buttons on the outside of the iPad and use them to make the music louder or softer.

- Use the slider in the Music app, located in the upper-right part of the screen, to change the volume. See Figure 5-4.

To pause and restart a song, skip to the previous and upcoming song in the song list, and rewind and fast forward a song that's currently playing:

- While a song is playing, notice the controls at the top of the screen. See Figure 5-4.

Explore Views

You've been exploring the Music app's default screen so far. That's the light-colored screen with the tabs that run across the bottom and the controls across the top. Here you'll explore two other views available in the Music app: Album Art view and Track List view.

TIP

Purchase AirPlay-enabled speakers for your iPad and stream your music to them, without wires. Once you have the speakers set up, you'll see the AirPlay icon on the Music app.

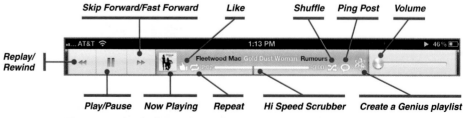

Figure 5-4: **Controls for managing playback are available at the top of the screen.**

QUICKSTEPS

SWITCHING VIEWS

To practice moving between Album Art view and Track view:

1. In any view, tap **Albums** at the bottom of the screen. If you see information about the tracks on an album, tap outside of it to hide it.

2. Tap an album name, and then tap a song on the album to play it to get the full Music app experience.

3. Tap the small thumbnail that appears at the top of the screen to access Album Art view. This is the Now Playing thumbnail.

4. Now in Album Art view, tap the screen once to access the controls.

5. Tap the icon in the bottom-right corner to switch to Track List view. Tap again to return to Album Art view.

6. Tap the thumbnail at the top of the page to return to the list that contains the songs on the album.

7. Continue experimenting as desired.

Album Art view is just that: it's a view that shows the album cover. While in Album Art view, you can tap once to access the playback controls (and tap again to hide them), and while the controls are showing, you can switch to other views easily, manage what's playing, and more. In Album Art view, you still have access to the tabs across the bottom too. Figure 5-5 shows this view and where to tap to access other views.

Track List view shows the list of songs in an album or playlist and how long each song is. Track List view allows you to switch to a different song in an album or playlist quickly, shuffle songs, replay songs, and more. You can see what's playing in the status bar at the top of the screen. You can use Track List view to manage audiobooks too. See Figure 5-6.

Tap to return to the previous view **Toggle between Album Art and Track List views**

Figure 5-5: In Album Art view you can tap to gain access to the controls; otherwise, all you see is the album art.

	The Lion, Witch, Wardrobe 01	C. S. Lewis	1:20
2	The Lion, Witch, Wardrobe 02	C. S. Lewis	10:07
3	The Lion, Witch, Wardrobe 03	C. S. Lewis	15:29
4	The Lion, Witch, Wardrobe 04	C. S. Lewis	12:08
5	The Lion, Witch, Wardrobe 05	C. S. Lewis	14:35
6	The Lion, Witch, Wardrobe 06	C. S. Lewis	13:51
7	The Lion, Witch, Wardrobe 07	C. S. Lewis	13:11
8	The Lion, Witch, Wardrobe 08	C. S. Lewis	16:34
9	The Lion, Witch, Wardrobe 09	C. S. Lewis	16:16
10	The Lion, Witch, Wardrobe 10	C. S. Lewis	16:26
11	The Lion, Witch, Wardrobe 11	C. S. Lewis	16:36
12	The Lion, Witch, Wardrobe 12	C. S. Lewis	16:38
13	The Lion, Witch, Wardrobe 13	C. S. Lewis	16:11

Figure 5-6: *Track List view offers information about what's next, how long each song is, and the song title and artist, among other things.*

NOTE

The first time you use Genius, you'll be prompted to enable the feature. If you've been using iTunes for a long time, you may not even remember doing this! If you've never enabled Genius, you'll be prompted to. Follow the directions if so.

Incorporate Playlists

The list of songs on an album is called a *playlist;* it's a list of songs to be played. You can create your own playlists and add any songs you like to personalize your music experience. In a personalized standard playlist, you get to hand-pick the songs to include. There's built-in support for creating playlists in the Music app. (Depending on your age, you may liken a playlist to an older type of music playlist of songs: the "mixed tape.") You can also create "Genius" playlists.

CREATING A PERSONALIZED PLAYLIST

A standard, or *personalized*, playlist is a playlist you create by manually selecting the songs you want to include in it. Once created, a playlist can be edited.

CREATE A STANDARD PLAYLIST

To create a standard playlist in your iPad's Music app:

1. Tap the **Playlists** option at the bottom of the Music interface.

2. Tap **New**.

3. Type a name for the playlist, and tap **Save**.

4. Tap the plus sign (+) to add the song. The song will appear grayed out after you tap it.

5. Tap **Done**.

6. If desired, tap **Edit** to edit the playlist. You'll learn more about this in the next section. If not, tap **Done**.

EDIT A PLAYLIST YOU'VE CREATED

To edit a playlist:

1. Tap the playlist you want to edit, and then tap **Edit**. (If you're working from the previous set of steps, skip to Step 2.)

2. To move a song up or down in the list, tap, hold, and drag the three gray bars at the far right of the song info to the desired location, and then drop it there.

Continued . . .

Genius analyzes your music library and draws conclusions about what type of playlist you'll like, based on a single song you pick.

Create a Genius Playlist

You can create a Genius playlist by tapping a song you want to base the list on and tapping the Genius icon.

1. Tap **Music** to open the app.

2. Tap a song to be the basis for the playlist. It will begin to play.

3. With a song playing, and from any screen, tap the **Genius** icon. The icon may appear on a gray background or a black one, depending on the current view.

4. If there is enough information for Music to draw from, a new Genius playlist will be created.

5. To see the playlist:

   a. Tap **Playlists** at the bottom of the page.

   b. Tap any applicable "back" buttons to get to the Playlist view.

   c. Note the new playlist.

6. Tap the playlist to view it.

7. Tap **Save** to save the playlist, or tap **Refresh** to refresh it with new songs.

8. Once a playlist is saved, you can edit it using the resulting Edit button.

Play a Playlist

You tap a playlist to access it, and tap a song in it to play it. When you play songs in any list, they play from top to bottom, or from start to finish, no matter what the source of the list. You may want to *shuffle* those songs so they play in random order, especially if this list is in alphabetical order or if the songs in the list are grouped by artist or album. Just tap the shuffle button in any playlist.

3. To delete any song, tap the red circle on the left side of the song name. (Deleting a song from a playlist doesn't delete it from your iPad.)

Playlists	Party Tunes		Add Songs	Done
	4 Songs, 19 Mins			
⊖ 1. All I Wanna Do	Crow, Sheryl			≡
⊖ 2. Galileo	Indigo Girls	Rites of Passage		≡
⊖ 3. Bad	Michael Jackson			≡
⊖ 4. Ghost	Indigo Girls	Retrospective		≡

4. To add more songs, tap **Add Songs**, tap the songs you want to add, and then tap **Done**.

5. Tap **Done** again.

6. Tap **Playlists** to return to the Playlists screen.

TIP

You can delete a playlist. Just press and hold the playlist and tap the black X that appears on it. The songs in the list will remain on the iPad.

TIP

You can create a "smart playlist" in iTunes on your computer that contains your top-rated or favorite songs. You can also create smart playlists that contain the songs you play the most. Smart playlists are just that; they're smart and update themselves as your tastes change and as criteria for the playlist are met.

To play a playlist:

1. In the Music app, tap **Playlists**.

2. Tap a playlist.

3. Tap any song in the list to play it.

Sync Playlists

When you connect your iPad to your computer or sync it wirelessly, playlists you've created on your iPad will sync to your iTunes Music Library on your computer. You'll see the playlist in two places in iTunes: in the source pane under Playlists, and when your iPad is selected, under the Music tab. Alternatively, you can opt to select only specific playlists to sync by selecting them under the Music tab, as shown earlier. Finally, you can create playlists in iTunes at your computer and include those too.

Stream Your Music

You can access music that's currently stored in your computer's iTunes library from your iPad over your home Wi-Fi network. This means that while you're at home and connected to your Wi-Fi network from your iPad, you'll be able to access the music in your library (the media stored on your computer) without having to actually put that media on your iPad. This will save space on your iPad because you won't have to sync all of your music to have access to it. Likewise, you can share the music on your iPad with devices on your Wi-Fi network.

To make this happen, you must first enable home sharing from your iPad. Basically, you tap **Settings**, tap **Music**, and type your Apple ID and password under Home Sharing.

Next, you must enable Home Sharing from iTunes at your computer. Click **Advanced**, and click **Turn On Home Sharing**, shown in Figure 5-7. Type your Apple ID and password, press ENTER, and tap **Done**.

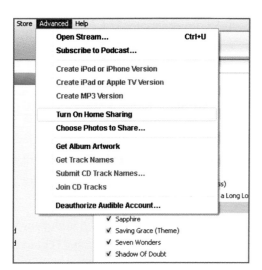

Figure 5-7: *Enable Home Sharing from iTunes.*

Figure 5-8: *From iTunes, you can decide what to share.*

You can also select what to share. In iTunes, from your computer, click **Edit** and click **Preferences**. Click **Sharing**. Configure what you want to share, as shown in Figure 5-8. You'll notice that Pictures is not an option. However, music, podcasts, playlists, videos, and the like are options for sharing.

Now, open the Music app on your iPad, and tap **More**. Tap **Shared**, which only appears if you've configured both your iPad and iTunes to share media. When you tap Shared, the results include the option to play music from what's stored on your iPad or from what's stored on your shared library. To switch to your shared library, select it.

Now what's available from your iPad's Music app includes what's been shared from your local network. As you can see here, this may really open up your iPad to a lot more music! As you can see in Figure 5-9, letters now appear on the right side because there is so much music available.

The more you experiment with Home Sharing, the more you'll uncover. As an example, in the Videos app, you'll notice there's a new Shared tab (provided you opted to share this media). Tapping the tab offers access to the shared video media on the computer. What you see here will depend on what kinds of videos you have on your home network and what you decided to share.

Consider iTunes Match

iTunes Match is another method you can use to make music available on your iPad. When you pay for the service (about $25 a year), any songs you've purchased from Apple will be available in iCloud, as you'd suspect, but any other songs you have in your library (ripped from your personal CD collection, for example) will be matched to what's in Apple's vast online media library. All of those songs, assuming a match can be found, will be available from iCloud at 25Kbps AAC DRM-free quality, even if your original copy was of a lower quality. Any songs you have that Apple can't match will be copied and be available to you through iTunes Match at their original quality. You can store up to 25,000 songs in iTunes Match, and this data doesn't count against the iCloud storage you have for other uses.

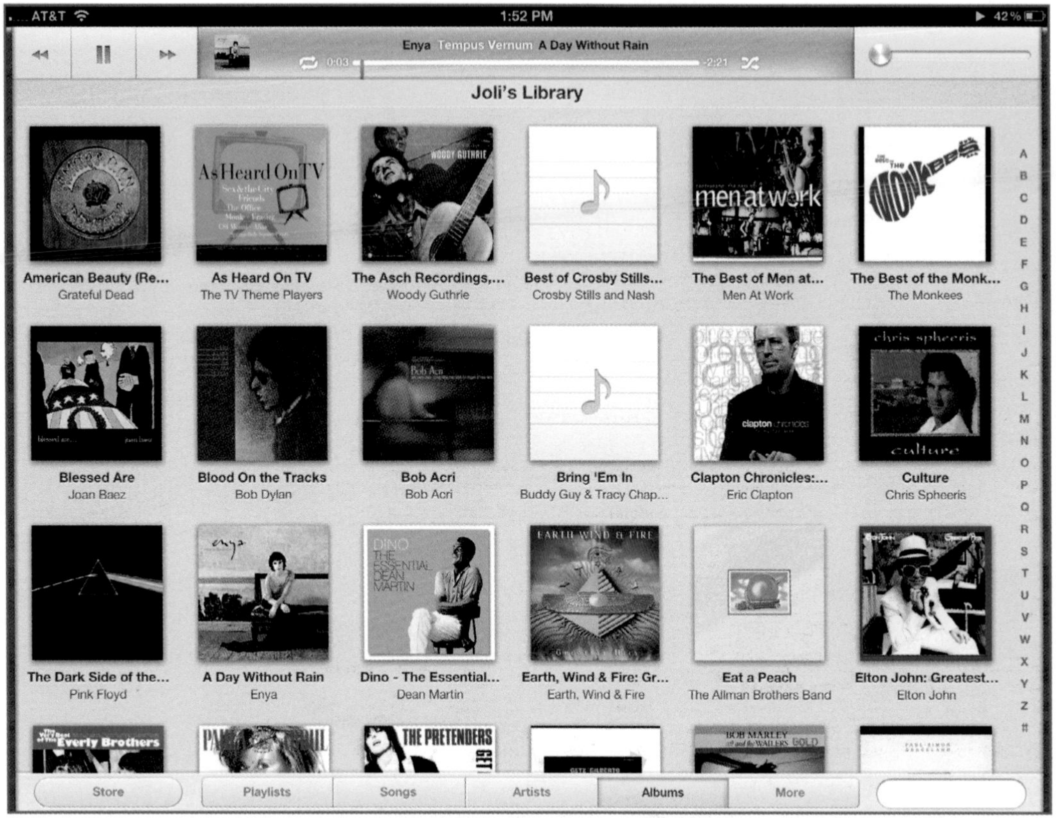

You turn on iTunes Match from your iPad (select **Settings | Music | iTunes Match**). When you do, all your music is available to you without filling up your iPad. When you select a song to play, the song will be downloaded onto your iPad. The cloud icon by the song name disappears after the song is downloaded. Read more about iTunes Match here: http://www .apple.com/itunes/itunes-match.

iTunes Match is similar to Home Sharing, only you don't have to be at home on the same network as your computer. If you turn on cellular access in Settings, you can stream these songs over Wi-Fi or cellular service. Playlists you create will be shared with other iTunes Match users on your account (up to ten devices are supported, including your home computer).

Figure 5-9: When you make your shared libraries available from your home network, you increase the size of your Music Library while connected to it.

NOTE

Your computer will have to be turned on, with iTunes active, for sharing to work properly.

Chapter 6
Shopping iTunes, the App Store, and the iBookstore

You may have music, movies, audiobooks, and other data on your computer that you can sync to your iPad, but may not have apps, podcasts, digital books, magazines, the latest music video, or a copy of last week's airing of your favorite TV show (unless you own or have owned other iDevices). That's what this chapter is all about: obtaining different types of media from the Internet, getting that media on your iPad, and using it. You can obtain this media in many ways, including using iTunes and using the App Store, both options on your iPad.

Shop with iTunes

The iTunes Store is a one-stop shop for music, movies, TV shows, podcasts, audiobooks, and even college lectures from universities all over the country. You can preview and buy just about any kind of media imaginable. And, as with other iPad media, it's easy to sync your newly acquired media to your desktop computer. You can also access (and redownload) purchases directly from your iPad using the iTunes and App Store apps (and from the iBookstore). Just click the Purchased tab to see what's available. Purchases you make from Apple are stored automatically in iCloud.

Once you've acquired media from the iTunes Store, you'll use other apps to view it or listen to it. You listen to music, audio podcasts, and audiobooks with the Music app. You can watch movies, music videos, video podcasts, and TV shows with the Videos app. And you can listen to proprietary media in other places, too; you can listen to Audible audiobooks from the Audible app, for instance. Figure 6-1 shows the iTunes interface.

Understand the iTunes Interface

When you enter the iTunes Store (by tapping the iTunes icon on your iPad), you have access to various buttons to help you navigate iTunes. These options help you sort the media by its type and then narrow down the results.

CHOOSE A MEDIA CATEGORY

The categories across the bottom of the page help you navigate iTunes by making sorting options available. Tap any category button to show only media in that category:

- **Music** Find music from just about every artist imaginable.
- **Movies** Buy or rent movies, access new releases, and access free movie previews.
- **TV Shows** Purchase entire seasons of shows or a single show. Once purchased, those shows belong to you and can be stored on your iPad, in iCloud, or on your computer.

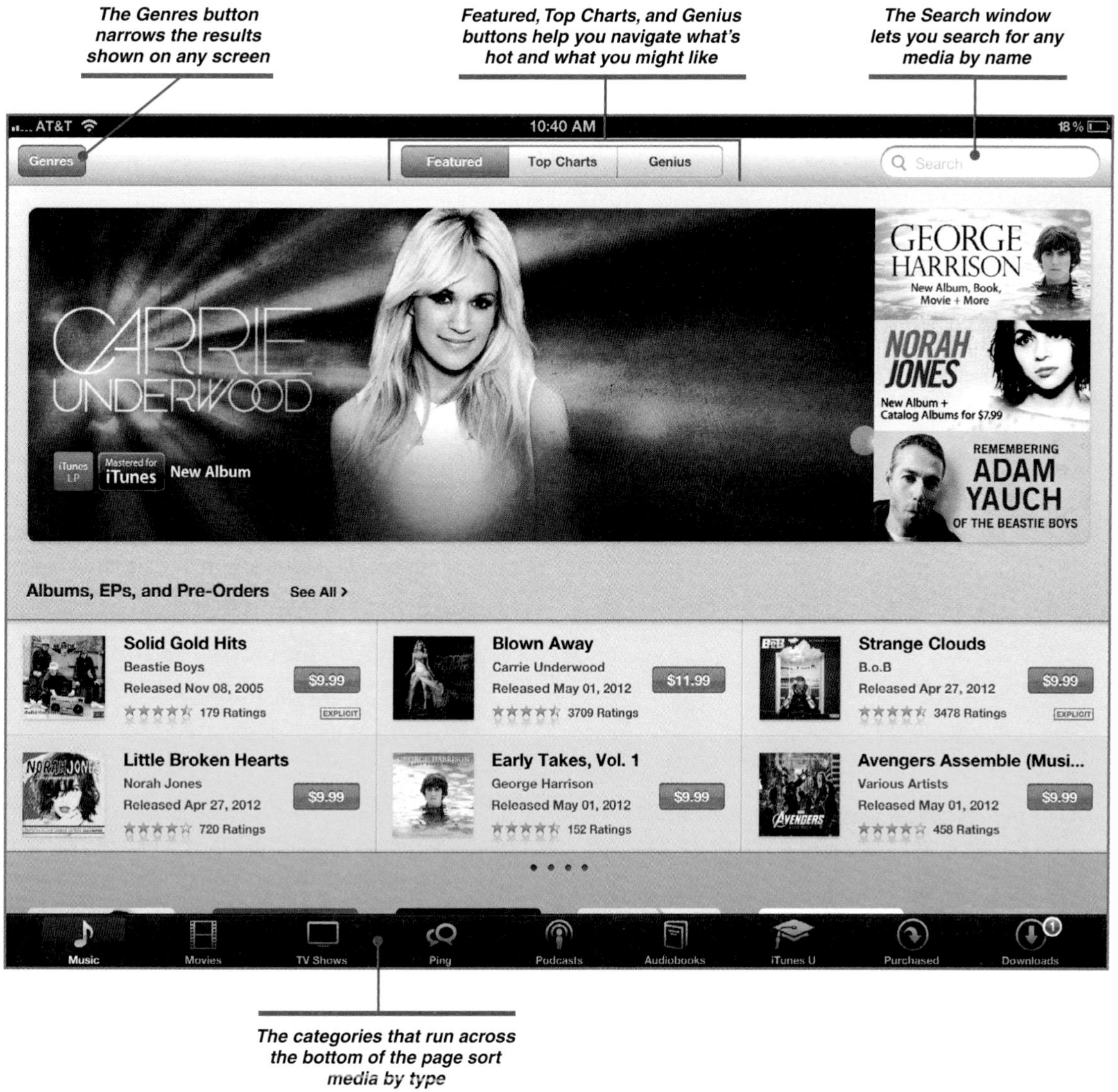

The Genres button
narrows the results
shown on any screen

Featured, Top Charts, and Genius
buttons help you navigate what's
hot and what you might like

The Search window
lets you search for any
media by name

....AT&T 🛜 10:40 AM 18%

Genres   Featured Top Charts Genius   Q Search

GEORGE HARRISON
New Album, Book, Movie + More

NORAH JONES
New Album +
Catalog Albums for $7.99

REMEMBERING
ADAM YAUCH
OF THE BEASTIE BOYS

iTunes LP   Mastered for iTunes   New Album

Albums, EPs, and Pre-Orders   See All >

Solid Gold Hits
Beastie Boys
Released Nov 08, 2005 $9.99
★★★★☆ 179 Ratings   EXPLICIT

Blown Away
Carrie Underwood
Released May 01, 2012 $11.99
★★★★☆ 3709 Ratings

Strange Clouds
B.o.B
Released Apr 27, 2012 $9.99
★★★★☆ 3478 Ratings   EXPLICIT

Little Broken Hearts
Norah Jones
Released Apr 27, 2012 $9.99
★★★★☆ 720 Ratings

Early Takes, Vol. 1
George Harrison
Released May 01, 2012 $9.99
★★★★☆ 152 Ratings

Avengers Assemble (Musi...
Various Artists
Released May 01, 2012 $9.99
★★★★☆ 458 Ratings

• • • •

Music   Movies   TV Shows   Ping   Podcasts   Audiobooks   iTunes U   Purchased   Downloads

The categories that run across
the bottom of the page sort
media by type

Figure 6-1: *The iTunes interface offers a myriad of ways to browse media; here the Music category is selected.*

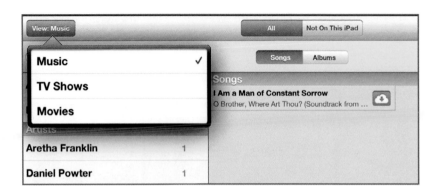

Figure 6-2: *All of your purchased media, even media purchased on an iPhone or iPod touch, is available from the Purchased button.*

- **Ping**   See what others are watching and listening to, and receive recommendations from them. To use Ping you must first enable it in iTunes and configure the settings, and then opt to follow someone, perhaps a friend or celebrity.

- **Podcasts**   Browse and obtain audio and video podcasts.

- **Audiobooks**   Browse and purchase audiobooks.

- **iTunes U**   Browse college lectures from universities (including Yale or Berkeley), browse K–12 offerings, and even watch videos taken in museums and television stations. You'll browse from the iTunes U app, technically.

- **Purchased**   Browse purchases by Music, TV Shows, and Movies. Figure 6-2 shows our purchases and the cloud icon. (You tap the cloud icon to download or redownload the purchase.)

- **Downloads**   See items you are currently downloading. Once the media has been downloaded, the list will be empty and data will be available in its associated app (music in the Music app, movies in the Videos app, and so on).

NARROW DOWN THE RESULTS

Once you're in the proper category across the bottom of the interface (Music, Movies, TV Shows, and so on), explore the media in it using the buttons that run across the top. Here are the buttons you may encounter:

- **Genres**   Tap this button to show the available genres at the iTunes Store when you're in the Music, Movies, or TV Shows category. The genres change depending on what you've selected across the bottom of the screen. For instance, if you're browsing TV Shows, the Genres button produces All, Animation, Classic, Comedy, Drama, Kids, Nonfiction, Reality TV, Sci-Fi & Fantasy, and Sports. If you're in Movies, Genres include some of those and others like Thriller and Documentary. (Tap Genres again to hide the list, or tap outside of it.)

- **Categories**   You'll see Categories where Genres was in the previous bullet when you tap Podcasts or Audiobooks across the bottom. Categories include Comedy, Fiction, History, News, and the like.

- **View**   You'll only see the View option when you've selected Purchased at the bottom of the iTunes interface. You can choose from Music, TV Shows, and Movies.

- **Featured**   Tap Featured, available in almost every category, to view media that Apple thinks is noteworthy. The items listed here are handpicked by Apple. Depending on

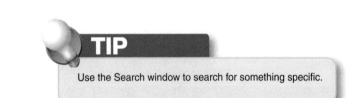

TIP

Use the Search window to search for something specific.

the category you're in (TV Shows, Movies, Music, and the like), you'll see options under Featured such as "Latest TV Episodes" or "New Releases." You can flick to move left and right among the listings. There's also an option to "See All."

- **Top Charts** Tap Top Charts to see the most popular media at the moment for a specific category. This list will change often as the top sellers change. What's hot today may not be hot tomorrow!

- **Genius** Tap Genius (when available) to see if iTunes has any Genius suggestions for you. Genius will compile information about your preferences as you download media, and then offer recommendations for other media you might like (see Figure 6-3). Genius bases its recommendations on what you've previously purchased or sampled. If you purchase a specific genre from the Top Charts listings in the music category, Genius will suggest similar songs in that genre as they are released. If you prefer show tunes, for example, Genius may well suggest movie soundtracks and Broadway releases.

Browse and Buy Music

The best way to become familiar with the iTunes Store is to browse music. Open iTunes and touch **Music** to get started. You'll see several panes, boxes, and lists, most of which were detailed previously. Tap these to explore more. Next, scroll to the bottom of the music's Featured page to see Quick Links, where you can access Free On iTunes, Music Videos, and more.

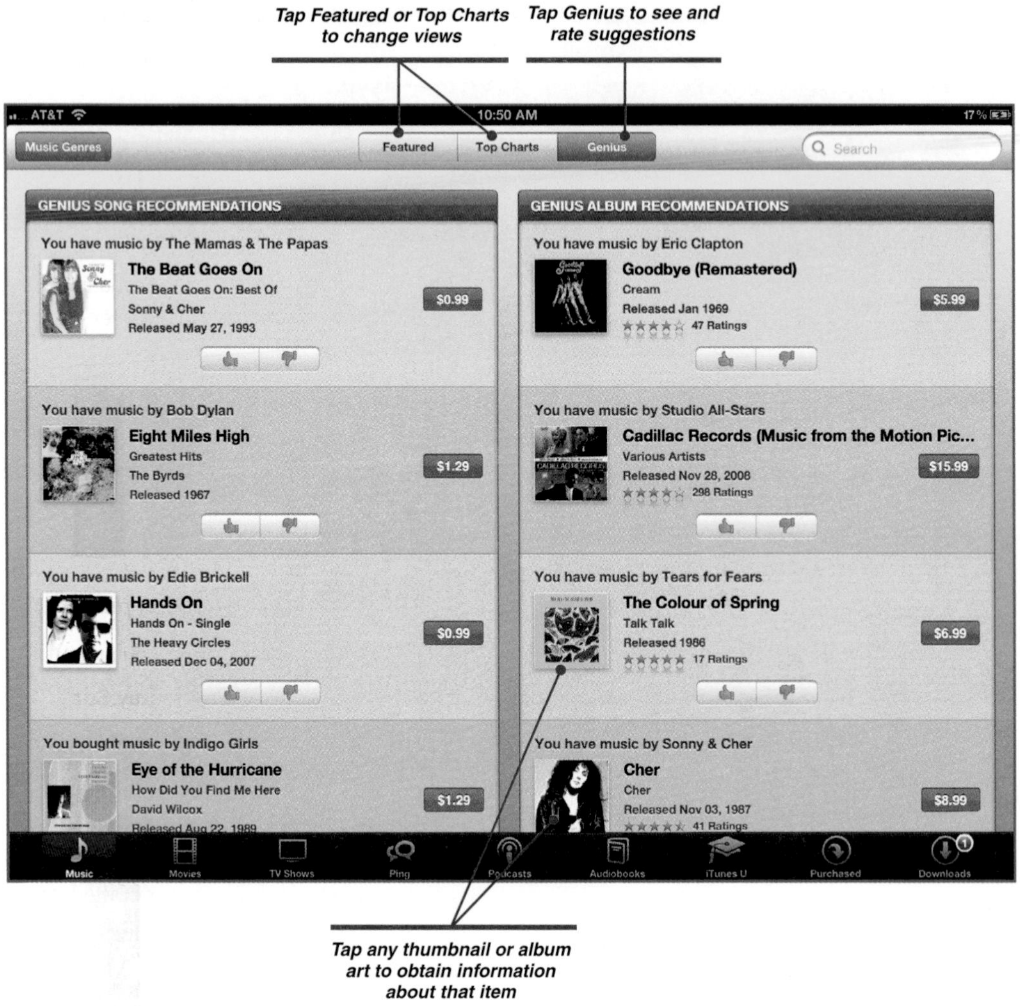

Tap Featured or Top Charts to change views

Tap Genius to see and rate suggestions

Figure 6-3: *Genius bases its suggestions on what you've previously purchased.*

Tap any thumbnail or album art to obtain information about that item

In any music-related page, you can tap Genres to cull down the media to a specific type for that page. For instance, if you're in the Top Charts category of music and you only want to see songs that are considered "country," touch **Genres** and choose **Country**, as shown in Figure 6-4. The list will change and

Figure 6-4: *You can sort any music page by genre to narrow down the results for a category.*

only supply the top songs in that category. Continue to experiment with other categories and sort by Rock, Pop, or Reggae, for instance.

Sometimes you know exactly what you want. You can use Search inside the iTunes Store to search for a specific song or album.

1. Tap inside the Search box in the top-right corner.
2. Type the artist's name, a song name, or other identifying information.
3. Tap **Search** on the keyboard or, if the result appears in the list (shown in the following illustration), tap that to see the search results.

When you're ready to purchase a song or album:

1. Locate the price button and tap it.
2. Tap **Buy Album** or **Buy Song**.
3. Type your password and tap **OK**.
4. Close iTunes and open the Music app to play the song.

TIP

The Music app was detailed in Chapter 5.

Figure 6-5: **When buying TV shows, you can often buy the entire season or a single episode.**

Browse and Buy Movies

Your new iPad can play high-definition (HD) movies as well as standard-definition movies, which you can rent or buy from the iTunes Store. You may never have purchased a movie from your iPad, but you browse and buy or rent movies in the same manner as you browse and buy music.

1. Tap **iTunes** to open it.
2. Tap **Movies**.
3. If desired, tap **Featured**, **Top Charts**, or **Genius**.
4. If desired, tap **Genres** and tap any genre listed.
5. Tap **View** to get more information about the movie.
6. Tap **Preview**, if desired, to preview the movie.
7. The Buy option must be available to purchase the movie. It is possible only Rent is an option (in this case, see the QuickSteps "Renting a Movie"). Tap **Buy** to buy a movie.

Browse and Obtain Other Media

There are other types of media, as detailed earlier. Specifically, there are TV shows, podcasts, audiobooks, and media from iTunes U (iTunes University).

OBTAIN TV SHOWS

You browse for and buy TV shows the same way you browse for and buy music and movies. With TV shows, though, you often have the option to purchase the entire season or a single show. See Figure 6-5.

OBTAIN PODCASTS

A podcast is an audio or video recording that has been made available to the public. Often podcasts are created by smaller entities than TV shows and movie makers. In the Podcasts section you may find "Indie" type subjects, offerings from NPR, newspapers, and news broadcasts, and even podcasts from ordinary people, stating opinions on sports, health, or other subjects. The best way to get a feel for podcasts is to touch the Podcasts button, look for a free podcast, and download an episode or two. Podcasts, once downloaded, can be played in the Music app or the Videos app, depending on what type of podcast you downloaded.

OBTAIN AUDIOBOOKS

Audiobooks are digital books that someone, perhaps the author or an actor or actress, reads aloud. You can purchase audiobooks in the same manner as you purchase music, movies, and other data. As with some of the other tabs, you can tap the Categories button to filter the results.

Use iTunes U

From the iTunes U tab, you can access audio and video files related to learning and higher education. Here you can obtain media to help you learn a new language or a new skill, or even listen to lectures given previously at Yale, Stanford, Berkeley, and other universities.

To obtain and listen to free media you find in iTunes U:

1. Tap **iTunes** and then tap **Open the iTunes U App**. (You could also just tap the iTunes U app, if you have it.)

2. Browse to locate the media you want to obtain. Look for the video icon by some offerings, denoting that the media is a video.

3. Tap the icon to access the Details page.

4. Tap **Free** and tap **Download**.

5. Tap the **Downloads** tab to follow the download process, if desired.

6. Once downloaded, close iTunes.

Figure 6-6: **Use the Videos app to view videos you download from iTunes U, music videos, podcasts, and more.**

You have a few choices for locating iTunes U media and playing it. If it's audio, you can open the Music app and listen to it there. If it's a video, you can look in the Videos app, under the appropriate tab. Figure 6-6 shows the Video app and the iTunes U tab.

Beyond navigating manually, though, it's important to note that anything you get from iTunes U shows up in your bookshelf in the iTunes U app, the way digital books appear in iBooks. (If you don't see the iTunes U app on your iPad, you can get it from the App Store.) This means that you don't really have to open the Music or Videos apps to find and play your content—you can just go to the iTunes U app and select whatever you want from your bookshelf. The app will handle opening up the correct application to play your video or audio. (Textbooks are also available in iTunes U. However, textbooks are downloaded into iBooks; they don't show up in the bookshelves in the iTunes U app.)

Get Apps from the App Store

The App Store is available from the App Store icon on the Home screen. Apps are programs you run on your iPad to perform specific tasks. You can get an app that helps you keep track of your workouts and weight loss, stay on top of breaking news, compare prices, or update your status on a social network, like Facebook, among other things.

Like iTunes, the App Store is configured with categories that make it easy to navigate. New, What's Hot, and Release Date run across the top, along with a Search option. Featured, Genius, Top Charts, Categories, Purchased, and Updates run across the bottom. Figure 6-7 shows these features.

TIP

You must be connected to the Internet to access any of Apple's stores.

See All *enables you to see all of the apps in a category*

The purchase price *changes to a Buy button when you tap it*

Thumbnails *enable you to access the Details page for an app*

Categories *lets you navigate the App Store by app type*

Purchased *lets you access previously purchased or free apps you've acquired*

Updates *lets you obtain app updates as they become available*

Figure 6-7: **The App Store offers various tabs for browsing.**

TIP

That plus sign (+) you see on some of the Free or price buttons means that there is a single version of the app that's designed both for the iPad and the iPhone.

Explore Apps

To open the App Store and explore all apps:

1. From the Home screen, tap **App Store**.

2. Tap **Featured** at the bottom, and tap **What's Hot** at the top. See Figure 6-8.

3. Continue exploring as desired, by tapping categories and options.

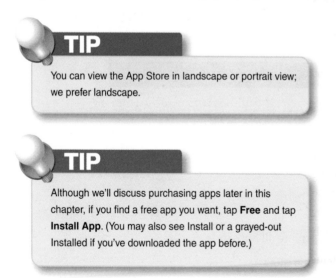

Figure 6-8: *Find out what's trending by looking at What's Hot.*

TIP

You can view the App Store in landscape or portrait view; we prefer landscape.

TIP

Although we'll discuss purchasing apps later in this chapter, if you find a free app you want, tap **Free** and tap **Install App**. (You may also see Install or a grayed-out Installed if you've downloaded the app before.)

If you don't want to buy an app, you can sort what's available in the App Store by what's free. There are free versions of games like Solitaire, practical apps like calculators, and apps that let you play a virtual guitar or piano. There are media apps from companies like Netflix, Time Warner, and ABC, and free versions of the most popular games, like Angry Birds or Draw Something.

To find popular and free apps for your iPad:

1. Touch the **App Store** icon on the Home screen.
2. Tap **Top Charts** at the bottom of the page.
3. Note how the apps are arranged. At the top are the Top Paid iPad Apps, and toward the middle, the Top Free iPad apps, and if you scroll down (flick up), the Top Grossing iPad Apps.
4. Tap **Categories** at the top of the page to filter the apps by type. You may want to filter by Health & Fitness, for example.

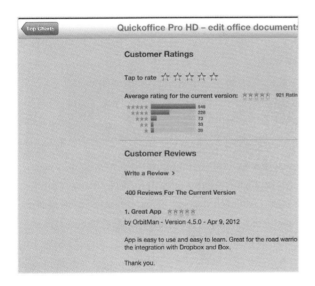

Read Reviews of Apps

You should always read the reviews of apps before you purchase them. While an app may look good on an iPhone and have many excellent reviews, it may lose its luster on an iPad. In addition, app reviews can reveal bugs with an app, problems contacting the manufacturer, or information regarding the value of the app in comparison to its price. Finally, reviews can help uncover any problems with the app, such as it being too violent or sexual (like a game), or not including information required to make it useful (which is often the case with reference apps).

Just about every app has a few reviews. Some have a ton. To find and read reviews for apps:

1. In the App Store, locate an app that you would like to learn more about.
2. Touch the app's icon, not the Free or price button.
3. Scroll down to the bottom of the information page, as shown in the illustration on the left, to access the ratings and other customer feedback.
4. Read any app review on the page, and if there are more than will fit on one page, touch **More**. Note that when a new version of an app is released, additional buttons become available to sort the reviews by version.
5. Tap the appropriate "back" button to return to the previous page.

Obtain a Newsstand App and Buy a Magazine

If you subscribe to a lot of magazines, you know what a pile you can acquire in only a few months. It's difficult to read them all, and even more difficult to throw them away. Moving from the printed version of a magazine to the digital version can resolve some of these issues. At the very least, you won't have to recycle them! And because you can take all of your magazines with you wherever you go, you may be more likely to read your magazines, too.

You acquire digital magazines (and newspapers) through the Newsstand app that's on your iPad's Home screen, although there are some exceptions to the rule. It's important to understand how the Newsstand app works before you jump in. Here's a brief rundown: The Newsstand app offers access to the

Newsstand Store. You tap the Store icon to enter. At the store, you browse the available magazine and newspaper apps. If you see an app for a publication you want to purchase or subscribe to, you download the free app for it. Then, back at Newsstand, you tap the app and make your purchase there, and after downloading it, read the magazine or newspaper there too.

You can take this one step at a time. To open the Newsstand Store:

1. From the Home screen, tap **Newsstand**. Your Newsstand will likely be empty (ours is not empty).

2. Tap **Store**.

Once in the store, you can browse the available magazine and newspaper apps, which are free, so it's okay to get one for the sake of experience. You don't get charged until you buy a publication through that app. You browse the magazine apps as you'd browse music, movies, podcasts, and other media. When you find a magazine or newspaper you think you'd like to purchase or subscribe to, install the app.

TIP

While reading a magazine or newspaper, press the **Home** button to return to the Newsstand app.

QUICKSTEPS

SEARCHING FOR AND BUYING AN APP

To purchase and download an app:

1. Locate the app you want to purchase in the App Store.

2. Tap the app to go to its Information page, if desired.

3. Tap the price of the app. (Alternately, tap **Free** and tap **Install App**.)

4. If applicable, tap **Buy App.**

5. Type your iTunes password, if prompted.

6. Watch the download process on your Home screen. Once the download is complete, tap the app to start it.

TIP

After you've used an app for a while, you may find that an update is available. You'll know when these updates are available because a number will appear on the App Store icon, and you'll see a number on the Updates tab of the App Store once it's opened. It's up to you whether or not to install updates. Always read the information offered about the update before installing it.

After you've downloaded an app for a magazine:

1. Tap the new app in the Newsstand.

2. If prompted to allow "push" notifications, read what's offered and tap **OK** or **Don't Allow**, as desired.

3. What you see now depends on the app, but all (or most) should offer an option to buy a single printing or edition, or subscribe to the magazine or newspaper. Explore the options; Figure 6-9 shows an example.

Use an App

The first time you start an app, you'll probably see an introductory screen that tells you how to use it. After bypassing that, you may then see a screen that prompts you to set up the app, like entering your name, age, or weight; providing a ZIP code or city; making a purchase (in the case of a Newsstand app); adding a player; or continuing where you left off the last time you used it. Because all apps are different, there's no way to be specific about what you'll see when you start an app and what you'll need to do to use it.

To start an app and use it:

1. Locate the icon for the app on the Home screen.

2. Tap the icon to start the app.

3. Read any introductory statements, and read any directions supplied.

4. Tap **Start**, **Play**, **Begin**, or another option. Once you've started an app, you may be prompted with instructions for play or use.

Get Books from the iBookstore

iBooks is a free app you obtain from the App Store that enables you to browse, download, and read digital books you obtain from the iBookstore. It's an easy

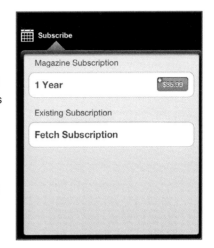

Figure 6-9: **Not all Newsstand apps behave the same; you'll have to explore each app independently to learn how to make a purchase or subscribe.**

way to turn your iPad into a fully functional e-book reader. You can also create bookmarks, look up the definitions of words, change the font size, adjust the brightness of the screen, and more.

Install iBooks

iBooks isn't installed by default; you have to get it from the App Store. (Technically, it's now called iBooks 2, but you don't need to worry about that.) It's free, however; and since you have the option of reading free books too, you don't have to lay out any money to enjoy iBooks.

To install iBooks using your iPad:

1. Tap the **App Store** icon on the Home screen.
2. Tap **Featured** or **Top Charts** at the bottom of the screen.
3. Tap inside the **Search** window, and type iBooks. Tap **iBooks** in the results.
4. Tap **Free**, next to the iBooks icon.
5. Tap **Install**.

Browse the iBookstore

You must be connected to the Internet to browse the iBookstore. In iBooks, tap **Store** to enter. The interface offers tabs, buttons, and categories you're already used to. To browse books in the iBookstore:

1. Touch the **iBooks** app on the Home screen.
2. Tap **Store** in the top-left corner. (If you see Library and not Store, you're already in the iBookstore.)

3. Tap **Featured** to view featured books.
4. Tap **Top Charts** to see a list of top paid and top free books.

5. Explore other options as desired.

6. Tap **Library** to return to iBooks.

Explore the New York Times Bestseller List

When you view a book's Information page, a new "back" button will appear; tap it to return to the previous screen.

TIP

One of the tabs in the iBookstore is NYTimes. The results are separated into fiction and nonfiction. You can scroll through the list by flicking up and down and left and right, and you can learn more about a book by tapping its icon. (You can also type a book title or author name to find a specific book.) When you tap a book's cover icon, the resulting page offers information about the author, customer reviews, and a description of the book, among other things. Figure 6-10 shows the NYTimes tab.

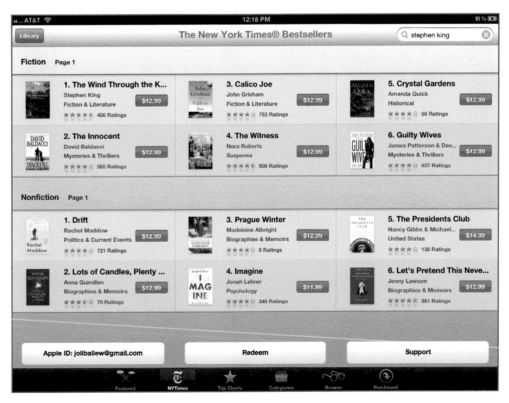

Figure 6-10: **The NYTimes tab offers an updated list of the most-popular-selling books at the moment.**

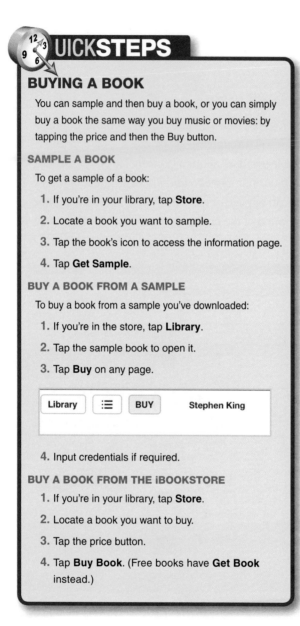

UICKSTEPS

BUYING A BOOK

You can sample and then buy a book, or you can simply buy a book the same way you buy music or movies: by tapping the price and then the Buy button.

SAMPLE A BOOK

To get a sample of a book:

1. If you're in your library, tap **Store**.

2. Locate a book you want to sample.

3. Tap the book's icon to access the information page.

4. Tap **Get Sample**.

BUY A BOOK FROM A SAMPLE

To buy a book from a sample you've downloaded:

1. If you're in the store, tap **Library**.

2. Tap the sample book to open it.

3. Tap **Buy** on any page.

Library	☰	BUY	Stephen King

4. Input credentials if required.

BUY A BOOK FROM THE iBOOKSTORE

1. If you're in your library, tap **Store**.

2. Locate a book you want to buy.

3. Tap the price button.

4. Tap **Buy Book**. (Free books have **Get Book** instead.)

Sample a Book

From the Information page of any book, you can tap **Get Sample** to read a small portion of it. Parts you can preview include (as applicable to the book):

- Table of contents
- Acknowledgments
- Foreword
- A sample chapter or part of a chapter, or multiple chapters

To preview a book, click the **Get Sample** button inside the Information page. A sample will download and will appear in your library. It will have a "Sample" banner across it.

Read a Book

You'll find your digital books on the iBooks virtual bookshelf. If you've downloaded any PDFs, they are there, too, but you'll have to tap **Collections** and tap **PDFs** to get to them. (If you only see PDF files and not books, tap

Collections and tap **Books**.) iBooks keeps books and PDFs separate to make them easier to find and manage.

To open and read a book:

1. Tap **iBooks**.
2. Tap any book on your bookshelf to read it.
3. Hold the iPad in portrait or landscape view to view it as a single page or facing pages, respectively.

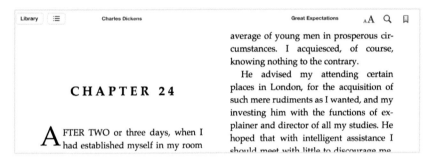

CHANGE THE FONT SIZE AND/OR BRIGHTNESS

To increase or decrease the font size:

1. Tap the **Fonts** button. It consists of two capital letters, both A, one small and one large.
2. To increase the font size, tap the large A. Tap again to increase the font size more. Repeat as desired.

3. To decrease the font size, tap the small A. Tap again to decrease the font size more. Repeat as desired.

To change the font, apply a theme, or view the book in full-screen mode:

1. Tap the **Fonts** button.
2. Tap **Fonts**.
3. Tap a font in the list.
4. Tap **Theme**.
5. Tap **Sepia** or **Night**, and then tap **Normal**, if desired.
6. Move the slider for Full Screen from Off to **On**. (This removes the book effects, including the simulated pages and binding.)
7. Tap outside of the menu to close it.

By default, your iPad will adjust the screen's brightness automatically. There's a sensor in the iPad that ascertains how much light is available and uses that information to make the adjustments. You can disable Auto-Brightness in Settings, under Brightness & Wallpaper, if you'd rather not have your iPad do this automatically. You can also change the brightness manually in iBooks while reading.

To change the brightness manually while reading a book in iBooks:

1. Tap the **Fonts** button.
2. Drag to reposition the brightness slider.
3. Tap anywhere in the book to close this control.

USING iBOOKS CONTROLS

You can read and navigate iBooks in various ways. If you need to access controls and they aren't showing, tap in the center of the page.

READ A BOOK

- **Turn a page**   Flick anywhere in the margin in the direction you wish to turn the page. Flick left to move forward in a book; flick right to move back. You can also tap in the margin in lieu of flicking.

- **Bookmark a page**   Tap the bookmark icon in the top-right corner. Bookmarks is an option in Contents as well, detailed later, allowing you to access your bookmarks quickly.

- **Highlight a word or phrase**   Tap and hold on the words you want to highlight. Drag from either end to highlight the text. Tap **Highlight**. (You can change the color of the highlight by tapping the highlighted text and selecting a new color from the list.) Explore Note and Search if you'd like.

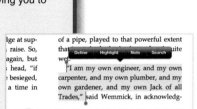

- **Define a word**   Tap and hold the word. Tap **Define** from the options that appear.

FIND A SPECIFIC PART OF A BOOK

To access the controls, they must be showing. Tap in the center of any page to show them (or hide them).

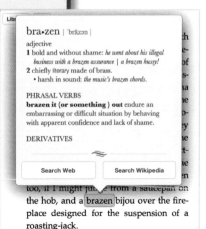

- **Move to a specific page**   Drag the slider to the desired page. Let go to jump to that page in the book.

Continued . . .

Manage Your Library

After you've used iBooks for a while, you may discover that you have too many books on your bookshelf and need to remove some. You may have so many books that you need to sort your books by their titles, authors, or category to find the book you want. You may even want to reorder the books on your bookshelf, placing the books you want to read in the order you plan to read them or create a new "collection" to hold them.

To sort books by their titles, authors, or categories:

1. Tap the **List** icon in the library. If you're in a book now, tap **Library** first.
2. At the bottom of the page, tap **Bookshelf**, **Titles**, **Authors**, or **Categories**.

To reposition the books on your bookshelf:

1. Tap the **Thumbnail** icon. The Thumbnail icon is to the left of the Edit and List buttons and consists of four small squares.

2. Tap and hold **Edit** until the book enlarges a bit.
3. Drag-and-drop the book to a new position on the bookshelf.
4. Repeat as desired and click the **Done** button when finished.

To delete a book:

1. In any view, tap **Edit**.
2. Tap **Delete** and then tap each book you want to delete.
3. Tap **Delete** again, and **Delete** to verify.
4. Repeat as desired and then click **Done**.

The library offers a button called Collections. Tap it to see the two available collections: Books and PDFs. The default view is Books, but if you download and need to access PDFs, you'll find them in the PDF collection. You can also

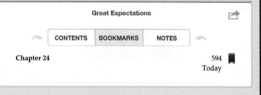
create your own "collection." Once created, you can move books there to organize them.

1. In Library view, tap **Collections**.

2. Tap **New**.

3. Type the name for the new collection. (You'll see other collections here if you've created them.)

4. Tap **Done**.

5. Repeat as desired.

6. Tap outside the collections window when complete.

To move a book into a collection you've created:

1. In Library view, tap **Edit**.

2. Tap a book to select it.

3. Tap **Move**.

4. Tap the collection you want to move the book to.

5. Note the new view with the book moved. Tap **Collections** to return to any other collection.

Chapter 7

Exploring More On-board Apps

You've been exploring apps throughout this book and have become familiar with many of them. Now it's time to explore some additional apps included with your iPad, specifically YouTube, Maps, Messages, and Game Center. Once you know how to use these apps, you can likely deduce how to use others.

Have Fun with YouTube

YouTube is a video-sharing website where users can upload and share videos they take or movies they create. Companies and artists also use YouTube to share clips of movies they produce, commercials they create for their products,

PLAYING YOUTUBE VIDEOS

To find a video to watch, browse the videos using the category buttons that run across the bottom of the YouTube window, or search for a specific video using the Search window. Tap any video to play it. The controls you'll use once a video is playing will look like controls you've seen in other apps. As detailed there, you can play, pause, fast forward, and rewind easily.

SWITCH BETWEEN MODES

Depending on several factors, your video may open in full-screen mode or it may only take up a small portion of the screen. You can easily switch between modes by pinching your fingers apart or together.

CONTROL PLAYBACK IN FULL-SCREEN MODE

Tap the video while in full-screen mode to access the available controls. They include Bookmark, Skip Back (to the start of the playing video), Play/Pause, and Skip Forward (to the end of the playing video). On the right is the option to change the view from full screen to its smaller counterpart. You can also access the hi-speed scrubbing slider at the top of the page to quickly locate a specific part of a video (not shown) and the volume slider at the bottom (shown).

CONTROL PLAYBACK IN HALF-SCREEN MODE

Tap the video while in the half-screen mode to access the available controls. These were introduced in Figure 7-1. Remember, you can move from half-screen to full-screen mode by pinching.

TIP

If you have an Apple TV, you can view YouTube videos on your HDTV and control playback. You'll see the AirPlay icon if you have the required setup.

TV show teasers, and music videos. However, most of the video on YouTube is created and uploaded by individuals.

You can access YouTube videos from the YouTube app on your iPad. You'll need to be connected to the Internet, either using free Wi-Fi or a generous cellular data plan. (If you have a limited data plan, make sure you're connected to a free network before continuing.) While you can browse all you want on YouTube without creating a user account, if you want to like or dislike videos, post comments, or perform similar tasks, you'll have to create one. (You'll also need a user account to upload videos from your iPad to YouTube.) For now, go ahead and browse without an account, and if you decide later that you need one, you can create one. Figure 7-1 shows one of the available views while in the YouTube app.

Search YouTube Videos

You have to be connected to the Internet to access YouTube. Because YouTube videos require that quite a bit of data be transferred, if you have a limited data plan, be careful how much time you spend here. Alternatively, you could connect to a free Wi-Fi network before continuing. That said, as with other apps, there are familiar buttons across the bottom:

- **Featured**   These are videos that are featured by YouTube because they're unique, meaningful, funny, or exhibit some other reason for featured status.

- **Top Rated**   When viewers view videos, they often rate them. The videos in this category are the highest-rated videos of the day, the week, and all time.

- **Most Viewed**   YouTube keeps track of how often viewers watch a video, and the videos in this category have more views than the others.

- **Favorites**   The videos here are ones you bookmark as videos you like. You can then access your favorite videos anytime you want. You will need to sign in with your YouTube account to access this feature.

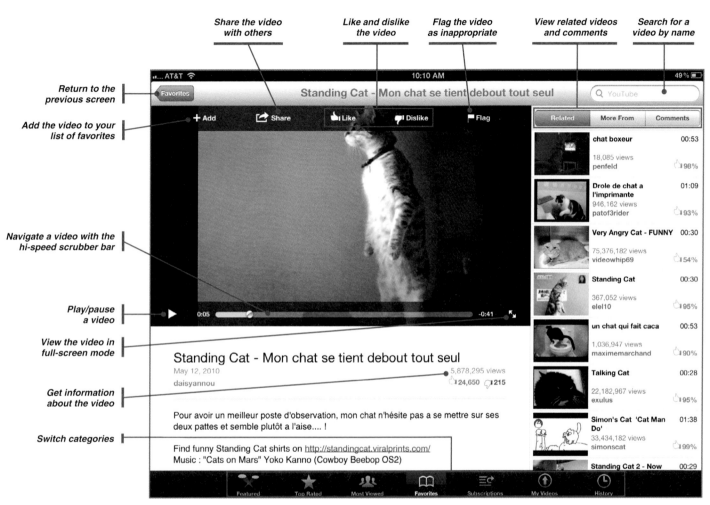

Share the video with others

Like and dislike the video

Flag the video as inappropriate

View related videos and comments

Search for a video by name

Return to the previous screen

Add the video to your list of favorites

Navigate a video with the hi-speed scrubber bar

Play/pause a video

View the video in full-screen mode

Get information about the video

Switch categories

Figure 7-1: *There are various views; this one offers almost all of the available features and tools.*

There's a Search window in the YouTube interface, and it works just like any Search window in any other iPad app, except that it doesn't offer a drop-down list of possible matches. Just tap it to type keywords for videos you'd like to see.

- **Subscriptions** If you like a particular YouTube user's videos, you can subscribe to them. You can then view all videos posted by that person easily, as well as any new videos they post. This requires a YouTube account. Figure 7-2 shows an example.

- **My Videos** If you've uploaded any of your own videos to YouTube, you'll have easy access to them here. You can also see how many people have viewed your videos and read any comments that have been posted. This requires a YouTube account.

Figure 7-2: *It's easy to subscribe to a person you like on YouTube.*

- **History**   The videos you've viewed on YouTube are listed here. This offers an easy way to access a video again, should you desire. You can tap Clear to remove your history entries.

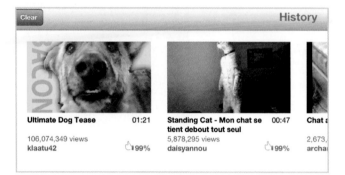

QUICKSTEPS

UPLOADING YOUR OWN VIDEO

You can take video with your iPad's video camera and upload it to YouTube, provided you have a YouTube account, and that the video is smaller than 2GB and is in an acceptable file format. You can also upload other video you have in the Photos app, perhaps video you obtained by uploading it using the optional Camera Connection Kit.

To upload video from your iPad to YouTube:

1. Tap the **Photos** app.

2. Locate the video and tap it. (If you recorded it with your iPad, it will appear in Albums, from Camera Roll.)

3. Tap the **Share** button, and tap **Send To YouTube**. (Sign in if required.)

4. Type a title and description, choose a quality setting, include tags, choose a category, and choose who can view the video (**Public** or **Unlisted**).

5. Tap **Publish**.

6. When prompted, tap **View On YouTube**, **Tell A Friend**, or **Close**.

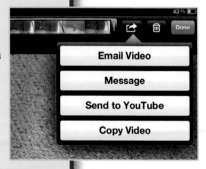

Rate and Comment on Videos

Once you have created your YouTube account and signed in, you're ready to like or dislike and comment on videos. Both are really easy, and both can be done from the smaller mode, discussed throughout this chapter.

To rate and comment on YouTube videos:

1. Locate a video you want to comment on, like, or dislike.

2. Pinch inward to access the smaller mode, if applicable.

3. Tap the video screen while in the smaller mode, and tap **Like** or **Dislike**.

4. Write your own comments in the Add A Comment window. Tap the **Send** key on the keyboard.

5. Tap **Flag** to let YouTube know you find the video offensive.

Share a YouTube Video

You can tap the Share icon (the arrow) to e-mail a link to a video to someone you think would enjoy it. Of course, you'll need to have Mail set up (see Chapter 4), and you'll need the e-mail address of the person you'd like to send the link to, but you probably already have all of that. When you tap Share, you can also opt to add the video to your Favorites or tweet it with Twitter.

Navigate with Maps

TIP

If prompted to enable Location Services, do so. It's the only way Maps will be able to find your present location, short of you typing it in the Start or End windows.

The Maps app offers directions to and from almost anywhere and the ability to share those directions easily with others. You can incorporate Maps with Google's Street View (when available) to view a picture of your destination, and you can access driving routes, walking routes, and public transportation routes easily. You can search for points of interest, landmarks, businesses, restaurants, or even a specific intersection. You can easily find your present location, and if a location isn't marked on a map, such as a friend's house or park, you can mark it yourself and save it as a bookmark. Figure 7-3 shows the Maps interface.

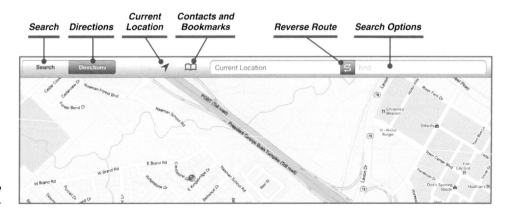

Figure 7-3: **The Maps interface has various buttons and icons.**

QUICK**FACTS**

UNDERSTANDING THE MAPS INTERFACE

You open the Maps app the same way you open any app: by tapping it once. There are several interface features to explore, and they are arranged familiarly with buttons and tabs.

THE TOOLBAR

The toolbar consists of the following options:

- **Search**   Tap Search when you want to view something specific on the map.

- **Directions**   Tap Directions to get directions from one place to another. You can type in a specific address, a business name, a location, and more.

- **Current Location**   Also called the arrow icon, tap this to show your present location on a map, orient the screen, or serve as a compass. What happens is dependent on how many times you've tapped it.

- **Contacts and Bookmarks**   Tap to see your contacts, the bookmarks you've saved, and to access them. Three tabs are available in the Bookmarks window:

  - **Bookmarks**   A list of bookmarks you've saved in Maps.

  - **Recents**   A list of places you've recently looked up with Maps.

  - **Contacts**   A list of the contacts you have in the Contacts app. You can tap any contact that has an address associated with it to access a map of the contact's location or to get directions to it.

- **The Search window(s)**   Type or dictate the name of a location, business, or geographic feature here to perform a search for it.

Continued . . .

Find Your Present Location

The best way to explore the Maps app is to first find your current location, and then tap the various options for views to see how they look. Because you're probably familiar with your surroundings, you can easily recognize what's around you when it appears on the map. Once the iPad knows your current location, you can easily browse nearby streets, businesses, and even the current traffic, if available.

To find your present location:

1. Tap **Maps**.

2. Tap the arrow icon shown here (it's next to the Bookmark icon).

3. Tap the blue dot that represents your location.

4. Tap the blue letter "i" to learn more about your location, including the address and the option to share your location with others, create a bookmark, and even view a picture, if available.

5. If you see a thumbnail, tap it. Then, tap the screen and tap **Done** to return to Maps.

6. Tap outside the Current Location box to hide it.

Now, touch the dog-ear located at the bottom right of the page to explore the various views. In any view, use your finger to scroll through the map. Finally, try these navigational techniques:

- Pinch your fingers toward each other to zoom out of a map.

- Pull your fingers outward to zoom in on an area on a map.

- Tap twice to zoom in. (Pinch to zoom back out.)

- Reposition the iPad from landscape to portrait view and back by turning the iPad 90 degrees left or right.

Get Directions

You can get directions in a number of ways. You can type (or dictate) any address to obtain driving directions to the address from your present location, and scroll through maps to view the terrain or route. If you need directions from one place to another but one of those places is not your current address, you can type in

QUICK**FACTS**

UNDERSTANDING THE
MAPS INTERFACE *(Continued)*

THE DOG-EAR

- **Standard**   View a graphical representation of the map with street names, parks, and water included.

- **Satellite**   View the location as it appears from the sky.

- **Hybrid**   View a map in Standard and Satellite view, together.

- **Terrain**   View the map in another graphical representation that includes terrain features, such as elevation. In this view you'll also see street names.

- **Traffic**   Show traffic conditions, if available, for the current map. Colors that denote traffic are red, yellow, and green.

- **Drop Pin**   Drop a pin anywhere on a map.

- **Print**   Print the map using a compatible AirPrint printer.

TIP

Remember, anytime you use the keyboard, you can dictate instead of type, if you've enabled the dictation feature in Settings and if you have an Internet connection. (You can't dictate passwords.)

NOTE

A ring will be drawn around the blue dot indicating your current location if your location couldn't be determined precisely. The smaller the circle, the more accurately the location was identified.

two addresses. This enables you to obtain directions from a starting point to an end point, from anywhere to anywhere.

To find an address and get directions to it:

1. In Maps, tap **Directions**.

2. Tap the **Location** icon to make sure Maps knows where you are.

3. To start from an address other than your current location, tap in that window, and type a new address.

4. Tap in the second window to type the ending address. You can also type a nearby business or other location.

5. Tap **Search** on the keyboard.

6. If applicable, tap the desired location, if more than one is available. See Figure 7-4.

7. At the bottom of the page, tap the driving icon. It looks like a car. (You can also tap the bus icon or the walking icon.)

8. Click **Start** and then advance through the directions using the arrow buttons.

*Figure 7-4: **When searching for something generic (like a park), you may see several entries.***

TIP

If you need directions to a location for a person or business that is stored in your Contacts list, tap the **Bookmark** icon and select the contact. Then, choose **Directions To Here** or **Directions From Here**.

TIP

If you'd like to invite others to meet you at a location, you can click **Share Location**, which is available on any information page. Tap it and then tap **Email**, **Message**, or **Tweet**.

Mark a Location

When you search for a restaurant or business (or something similar), Maps sets down a pin in its location. You touch the pin to get more information about it, including directions to it. Not all locations have pins, however. A brand-new restaurant won't, and neither will your home. You can add your own pins simply by tapping and holding an area of the screen.

To mark a location and save it as a bookmark:

1. Find the location on a map.
2. Tap and hold to drop a pin.
3. Tap the **i** to open the information page.
4. To name the location and save it, tap **Add To Bookmarks**, and name the bookmark as desired.

5. Tap **Save**.

Explore Street View

Street View is a view available via Google Maps that allows you to view pictures of a location or your destination. This feature provides 360-degree views of many locations across the world. You can access these images from the information window that appears in the pin associated with a location. (You have to tap the small "i" that appears when you tap the pin to get to this window.) When Street View is available, you'll see a thumbnail in the information window.

If you tap the thumbnail, you'll enter full-screen mode. While in full-screen mode, you can drag your finger across the screen to see what's to the left and right of the location, or even what's across the street. When you're finished exploring, tap the small icon in the bottom-right corner to return to Maps, as shown here (or tap the screen and tap Done).

TIP

To hide an information window, tap outside of it. To show it again, tap the pin on the map.

Share a Location via E-mail, Message, or Tweet

If you'd like to invite others to meet you at a location, you can tap **Share Location** from the information page. You'll see the option Share Location on every information page. Tap it to access the share options, which include Email, Message, and Tweet.

SENDING MESSAGES

To use the Messages app:

1. On the Home screen, tap **Messages**.

2. Tap the **Compose** icon.

3. Type the recipient's name in the To line, or tap the plus sign (+) to choose a contact from your list of contacts.

4. If the contact is a valid one, meaning they have an iOS 5 device and are using Messages, the name will turn blue in the To line. If they are not a valid contact, the activity icon will spin and eventually offer the red exclamation point you see here, and you'll have to press the X key on the keyboard to remove them.

5. Tap and type in the message field.

6. To add a picture, tap the camera icon and follow the prompts.

7. When you're ready, tap **Send**.

Use the Messages App

A Short Message Service (SMS) text is a short text message that's generally sent from one cell phone to another cell phone, and generally the recipient of the text sends one back. This exchange of words via cell phones is called *texting* and is (in this scenario) achieved over a cellular network like AT&T. When you use a cellular network to send texts, you generally have to pay for the privilege, either paying by the text or by the month.

TIP

There is now a Messages app for Mac, in beta, available for download at www.apple.com/macosx/mountain-lion/messages-beta.

There is no built-in way to send a text to any phone from your iPad (although third-party apps exist that can). However, the iPad does include the Messages app. This app makes it possible to send texts to your contacts if they also use certain iDevices. Those devices include iPads, iPhones, and iPod touches that use iOS 5. Texting with messages is free over Wi-Fi and it's unlimited.

Use Game Center

Game Center offers access to an online gaming network. Basically, it's an Apple-designed alternative to third-party matchmaking, leaderboard, and achievement-tracking services, which will only mean something to you if you're a big fan of gaming! In layman's terms, Game Center's purpose is to match up users who choose to play games against each other online, or to enable players to invite people they know or have previously met to play a game, and to let those players keep track of their scores and achievements.

You can also use Game Center to download games, review the status of the gaming friends you make, and see friend requests, among other things. You'll have to sign in with your Apple ID to get started and download games you want to play. After that, you're ready to compete!

Sign In to Game Center

If you've never used Game Center, tap the Game Center icon and provide your Apple ID and password to get started. You may have to provide your country and your date of birth, agree to some terms of service, create a secret word or question, provide the answer, create a nickname, or decide if you'd like to allow game invitations and other communications (you'll need to allow game invitations to play multiplayer online games). Once you've done all that, you're ready to play! See Figure 7-5.

Understand the Interface

You'll notice, after signing in, that there are four options across the bottom of the Game Center interface:

- **Me** This view shows your name, nickname, friends, games, achievements, and other information. You can type your status by tapping what is currently shown as "online." You can also tap any game's icon here to go to the App Store to get the game.

- **Friends** This view shows your friends, their status, and other information, and offers a way to add more friends.

Figure 7-5: **Open the Game Center and sign in to get started.**

- **Games** This view offers access to games you've recently played, your achievements, leaderboards, and a place to share news about a game with friends. You'll also see recommendations for new games you might like, based on games you've already bought.

- **Requests** This view offers information about friend requests and gives you the option to ignore, accept, or report a problem.

Get and Play a Game

There are several ways to find games, but one of the easiest is to open Game Center, tap **Games**, and tap **Find Game Center Games**. This will take you to the App Store where you can search for and download games as desired. Alternatively, you can tap the **Me** button and tap an icon for a game you recognize to go directly to that page in the App Store. Once you've downloaded a game, tap it on the appropriate iPad screen to start it, and work through any setup pages. You may see during setup that a game is Game Center–compatible.

Most Game Center–compatible games offer multiplayer modes, which bring up a Game Center matchmaking screen. This enables you to invite friends to play games with you. If you don't have enough friends to play against in a given game, Game Center includes Auto-Match, which will match you up against another player who's also interested in playing right now. When all players are ready, you can start playing together.

TIP

You can restrict your kids from playing online games or from being able to invite new people to play by selecting **Settings | General | Restrictions**.

TIP

It's important to note that a game must be "Game Center compatible" to be used effectively in the Game Center.

Chapter 8
Managing Contacts, Calendars, and Reminders

In this chapter you'll learn about three of the more practical apps available on your iPad: Contacts, Calendar, and Reminders. If you've ever used an e-mail program, cell phone, instant messaging program, or even an old-fashioned Rolodex, you're familiar with contacts. A contact is a person or company you, well, contact, via e-mail, phone, text message, instant message, letter, fax, or other medium. You're probably equally versed with calendars, too. Even if you've never used a digital calendar, you'll have no trouble adapting to the Calendar app on the iPad. Finally, you've likely written yourself short notes about tasks you need to

8

complete, and that's what the Reminders app is all about. Reminders offers a digital version of the common to-do list.

The best part about these three apps is that they're each iCloud compatible. This means that if you have additional iDevices and you configure iCloud properly, any change you make to a contact, calendar entry, or your reminders lists will be automatically pushed to those other devices. You no longer have to update them all separately, and thus, the information in these apps is always up to date. If you don't have other iDevices, that doesn't matter; iCloud gives you a place to back up this data safely and automatically. Beyond that, you can access your contacts, calendar, and even your reminders at www.icloud.com (whether you have other iDevices or not). This means you can check your calendar events at someone else's computer if you leave your iPad at home!

Communicate with and Manage Contacts

Your iPad comes with a Contacts app that allows you to keep digital contacts. When you add a contact manually, you can input the usual information: e-mail address, phone number, street address, ZIP code, and the like, but you can also add personal information, such as birthdays, anniversaries, and even children's names. You also can add a picture. Beyond adding the information, you can access contact information from various other apps, like Mail and Calendar. Figure 8-1 shows the Contacts app with a contact selected that has minimal information included with it. Tap the Contacts app to open it.

Figure 8-1: *The Contacts app has several interface features.*

Labels on the figure:

Search for a contact by name

Access grouped contacts

View an alphabetical list of contacts

Add a contact

Select a contact

Edit a contact

All Contacts

A
B
Stacey **B**
Jeff **Baker**
Joli **Ballew**
Joli **Ballew**
Joli **Ballew**
Joli **Ballew**
Joli **Ballew**
Lindy **Ballew**
Lucy Ballew
Pico **Ballew**
Barbara At Church

Lucy Ballew

notes

Share Contact

Edit

Add a Contact

You'll learn how to sync both contacts and calendar data in Chapter 9.

NOTE

You may or may not have any contacts in the Contacts app. You will have contacts if you've synced them from your computer, synced them from the cloud, or manually added them from Mail. If you've yet to take any of these steps, you can manually add a contact to get started.

Each entry available while editing a contact has a label. Phone entries may be labeled "work" or "mobile," for example. You can tap any label to make changes to its name or characteristics. In the case of a phone number, you may choose "work fax" or "main," among others.

Create a Contact

You can add various types of information to a contact, including a picture. Figure 8-2 shows a Contact card (in editing mode) with the keyboard hidden to show a few of the items you can add. There are more options available if you scroll down. Note the option at the bottom to link and unlink contact cards if more than one entry exists for a single contact.

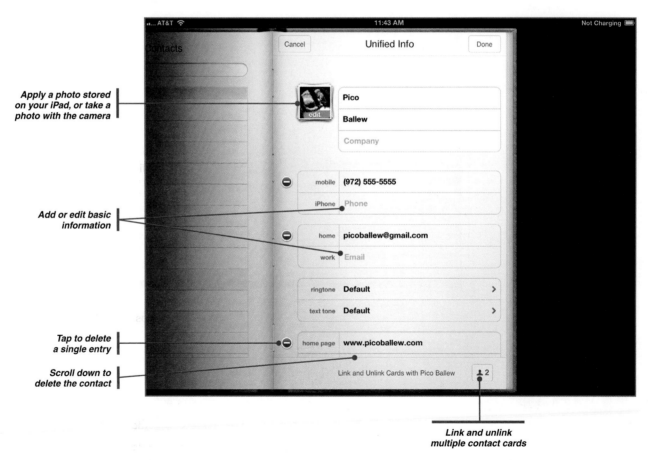

Apply a photo stored on your iPad, or take a photo with the camera

Add or edit basic information

Tap to delete a single entry

Scroll down to delete the contact

Link and unlink multiple contact cards

Figure 8-2: When you add a contact, you can include as little or as much information as you like.

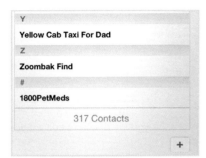

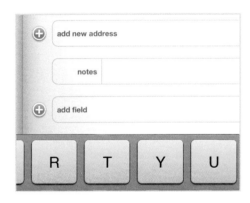

To add basic contact information:

1. Open the Contacts app.

2. Tap the plus sign (+).

3. Fill in basic information, shown in Figure 8-2, including but not limited to:

   a. First and last name

   b. Phone number

   c. E-mail address

   d. Street address

   e. City, state, and ZIP code

4. Leave the Contact card open.

To add other information:

1. Scroll down to the bottom of the Contact card, and tap the green plus sign next to Add Field. You can add several fields, including but not limited to:

   a. Prefix

   b. Phonetic first name

   c. Phonetic last name

   d. Nickname

   e. Job title

   f. Birthday

2. Depending on the option you chose in step 1, you'll have the option to input information regarding that field.

3. Leave the Contact card open.

To add a picture for a contact:

1. With a Contact card open, tap **Add Photo** in the top-left corner.

2. Tap **Take Photo** or **Choose Photo**.

3. Either tap the folder that contains the picture you want to add (and tap the picture you decide to use) or take a picture with the camera.

4. If desired, drag to move and scale the picture. Note that you can also pinch to resize it.

5. Tap **Use**; tap **Done**. The image will appear as shown, giving you the option to edit it if desired.

Locate a Contact

The Contacts app is one of the simpler apps to use. It looks like the physical address book you're probably already familiar with, and includes alphabetical tabs to let you access a page quickly. You can scroll through the contacts to locate the one you want.

1. Position the iPad in landscape view. (You can use portrait, but landscape is easier.)

2. Tap **Contacts** to open the app.

3. In the All Contacts list, flick up or down to scroll through the list; alternatively, tap any letter on the left side to go to that section of the Contacts list.

As your Contacts list grows, tapping a letter in the left margin and/or scrolling may not be the best way to locate the contact you want. If this happens, you can search for any contact in the Search window. You can use this window to type a part of your contact's name and view the results in a list.

To search for a contact:

1. In the Contacts app, locate the Search window.

2. Tap inside the Search window to bring up the virtual keyboard.

3. Type the first few letters of the name of the contact you'd like to find.

4. Tap the contact to view the Contact card.

QUICKSTEPS

GETTING A MAP TO A CONTACT'S ADDRESS

You can get a map to a contact's home or place of business quickly, provided you've previously input that address in the Contact card. To bring up a map:

1. Open the Contacts app.

2. Use any method desired to locate the contact.

3. Touch the contact to open their Contact card.

4. Touch the address.

5. Maps will open, and you can obtain the desired directions.

NOTE

You must enable Messages in Settings before you can use it. Select **Settings | Messages** and turn iMessage on.

TIP

If you receive an e-mail from someone you do not yet have in your Contacts list, tap the sender in the From line, and tap **Create New Contact**. Alternatively, you can tap **Add To Existing Contact**.

E-mail or Send a Message to a Contact

The main reason you add contacts on your iPad is almost always to make it easier to contact them. You may add yourself as a contact, too, so that you can easily share your contact information with others, and you may add a contact just so you'll have easy access to a map to their home. For the most part, though, you'll access the contacts when sending e-mails and messages. In both the Mail and Messages apps, you only need to type a few letters of the contact's name to access the contact information.

You have a couple of options for sending e-mail to a contact. You can open the Contact card for a person you'd like to communicate with in Contacts, and click their e-mail address to open a new message in Mail; or you can open the Mail app, start a new e-mail, and type part of the contact's name in the To line to add them there. Likewise, you can tap **Send Message** from any Contact card or type the contact's name in a new message from the Messages app to send a message.

To send an e-mail to a contact from the Contacts app:

1. Open Contacts and locate the contact you want to e-mail.

2. Tap their name to open their Contact card.

3. Tap their e-mail address to have Mail open automatically and insert the e-mail address in the To line.

To send an e-mail from the Mail app:

1. Tap **Mail** to open it.

2. Tap the **Compose** button.

3. Tap the plus sign to locate a contact you want to add, or type the first letter of their first or last name to select them from another list that appears (see Figure 8-3).

Figure 8-3: *You can send e-mail to a contact using the Contacts list.*

You send messages in the same manner. From inside the Contacts app, locate the contact and tap **Send Message**. Alternatively, you can tap the Messages app to open it, tap the **Compose** button, and begin typing the contact's name or tap the plus sign to access the Contacts list.

View Contacts at www.iCloud.com

You can enable iCloud for Contacts by selecting **Settings | iCloud** and access your contacts from just about anywhere. Just move the slider for Contacts from Off to On. Remember, though, you won't want to enable syncing with contacts on both your computer and iCloud; that will likely result in duplicate contacts on your iPad. However, once you've enabled iCloud for Contacts, if you decide to, you can access your contacts from any computer by navigating to www .icloud.com. See Figure 8-4.

Figure 8-4: If iCloud is enabled properly, Contacts, Calendar, and other iCloud data can be accessed from any computer that's connected to the Internet.

Beyond having access to your contacts from virtually any Internet-enabled device, iCloud also serves as a backup for your contacts. If you store your contacts here, you'll never again have to re-enter contacts manually should you lose or damage any of your iDevices.

Organize with Calendar

The Calendar app is available from the Home screen; tap it once to open it. If you haven't already synced existing calendar events through iTunes or iCloud, or subscribed to publicly available calendars, you'll only see an empty calendar. Figure 8-5 shows a populated Calendar app; this is Month view.

To open Calendar and explore the interface:

1. Tap the **Calendar** app on the Home screen.

2. At the top of the Calendar app, tap **Day**, **Week**, **Month**, **Year,** or **List**.

3. Turn the iPad 90 degrees to rotate from landscape view to portrait view.

Create a Calendar Entry

The best way to integrate the Calendar app with your iPad is to input some data. Think about all of the things you could input. To get started, you could create events for a few birthdays or an

Tap to show a list of any additional calendars you've configured or subscribed to

Tap to see invitations

Tap to change the view

Tap to search for something in Calendar

Tap to locate today on Calendar

Tap any month to go there quickly

Tap to add an event

Figure 8-5: **The Calendar offers various views and features to help you get and stay organized.**

NOTE

Remember you can lock the screen orientation if you prefer to always use a specific view.

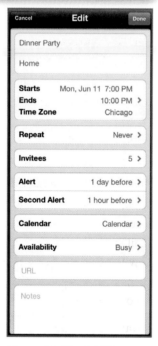

*Figure 8-6: **The Add Event window offers areas to input and configure information, dates, and times for the event.***

NOTE

You may not see all of these options (or you may see additional options) if you choose a calendar other than the iCloud Calendar. For instance, if you choose your Gmail calendar, Invitees and Availability will not appear.

anniversary, or anything you do every week or every month, such as an exercise class or dinner date. During the event creation process, you can also opt to add alerts. These alerts are essential if you don't plan to look at the Calendar app every day. When you create an alert, you'll get a pop-up message on your iPad and you can view them in the pull-down Notification list. The Add Event window is shown in Figure 8-6.

To add an event to the calendar and add alerts and reminders:

1. Open the Calendar app.
2. Tap the plus sign.
3. Type the desired information:

    a. **Title** Tap to add a descriptive title for the event. If you're adding a birthday, for instance, type <u>Cosmo's Birthday</u>.

    b. **Location** Tap to add a location, if applicable.

    c. **Start and end times** (or all-day event) Tap to configure the start and end times, or to create an all-day event. Note that when you tap this option, a new window appears. Click **Done** after entering the desired information.

    d. **Repeat** Tap to set the event to repeat. Choose from None, Every Day, Every Week, Every 2 Weeks, Every Month, or Every Year. Click **Done** when finished. Use the End Repeat setting to determine when an event no longer needs to repeat.

    e. **Invitees** Tap to invite people to the event by adding them from your Contacts list.

    f. **Alert** Tap to set an alert. Choose from None, At Time Of Event, 5 Minutes Before, 15 Minutes Before, 30 Minutes Before, 1 Hour Before, 2 Hours Before, 1 Day Before, and 2 Days Before. Tap **Done** when finished. If you set an alert, a new option will appear: Second Alert.

    g. **Calendar** Tap to choose a calendar, if more than one exists. What you see here will differ based on the calendars you have access to. When you add an event to a specific calendar, it will appear on that calendar. Click **Done** when finished.

    h. **Availability** Tap to change your availability. Options include Busy and Free.

    i. **URL** Tap to add a URL to an event, if the option appears.

    j. **Notes** Tap to type notes regarding the event.

NOTE

You can tap any entry and tap **Edit** to access any event's properties.

TIP

When you show multiple calendars from multiple sources, you may have more than one using the same display color. To change this, tap **Calendars**, tap **Edit**, tap the calendar you want to change, and then tap the desired color. Tap **Done** to apply it.

*Figure 8-7: **If you have multiple calendars, you may see more than one Add Calendar option.***

4. After all the information is added, tap **Done**.

5. Notice the new event on the calendar. Tap the event and tap **Edit** to edit the event, if desired.

	11
⊙ Dinner Party	7 PM

Create a Second Calendar

You can configure multiple calendars to manage your different responsibilities. You can create a calendar just for work, one for athletic endeavors, one for the hours you're responsible for taking care of an aging parent, and another to hold your children's sports schedules. Each calendar you create stands alone and can be viewed independently of the others. Each calendar has events listed in its own color, and each calendar can be viewed with any other calendar when needed.

You can create new calendars directly from your iPad. You can create additional calendars in the calendar application you use on your computer, too, and then sync them using iTunes. You can also include a calendar that you use with a related e-mail address (like Gmail or Yahoo!) by enabling them from the Settings app. You can also simply stick with the iCloud calendar and put everything there. When you opt for the latter, you can keep everything synced easily among all of your iDevices and have an online backup.

To create a new calendar from your iPad:

1. From the Home screen, tap **Calendar**.

2. Tap **Calendars** and tap **Edit**.

3. Tap **Add Calendar**. If you see more than one Add Calendar option, make sure to choose the desired "lead" calendar. See Figure 8-7.

4. Type the name of the calendar, and tap **Done**.

To include a calendar that is associated with an e-mail account like Gmail or Yahoo!:

1. From the Home screen, tap **Settings**.

2. Tap **Mail, Contacts, Calendars**.

3. Tap the e-mail account that has an associated calendar.

UICKSTEPS

SUBSCRIBING TO A THIRD-PARTY CALENDAR

To subscribe to a calendar available from Apple:

1. Tap **Safari** and navigate to www.icalshare.com.

2. Note the calendar categories.

3. Locate a calendar you'd like to include, and tap to select it.

4. Tap **Subscribe To Calendar**.

5. Tap **Subscribe**. Tap **Done**.

6. Open the Calendar app.

7. Tap **Calendars**.

8. Tap the new calendar to display it.

9. Tap outside the Calendar options window to close it, and note the new calendar entries.

TIP

Apple provides a number of free calendars if you'd like to try them out, including calendars for national holidays and sports events.

4. Turn on Calendars.

To sync a calendar that you keep on your computer:

1. Connect your iPad to your computer.

2. Select your iPad in the left pane of iTunes.

3. Click the **Info** tab.

4. Select **Sync Calendars With**, and select the calendar program you currently use.

5. Opt to sync all calendars or only specific calendars, and make the required selections.

Once you've added the desired calendars, on your iPad:

1. On the Home screen, tap **Calendar**.

2. Tap **Calendars** in the top-left corner.

3. If necessary, tap **Show All Calendars** (it will change to Hide All Calendars).

4. Note the new calendars.

You can now work with the additional calendars just as you worked with

a single one. Just remember that when you create new events, you need to choose the appropriate calendar to add it to. Also note that you can show and hide specific calendars if desired, to separate events and calendars.

Show Multiple Calendars

To view a single calendar and show multiple calendars at once:

1. In the Calendar app, tap **Calendars**.
2. Tap any calendar to show or hide it. If it has a check mark by it, the calendar will be displayed; if not, it will be hidden.

Subscribe to a Calendar

You can subscribe to compatible calendars on the Internet and have those events included with the calendar you keep on your iPad. You'll find calendars everywhere and for almost anything, including for your favorite sports teams, for your kid's lunch program at school, for work-related holidays, and more. To find calendars, perform a Google search for iCal Calendars for iPad.

Use Reminders

The iPad's new Reminders app is really a companion app for the Calendar app and the compatible calendars in it. It's a place to jot down or dictate checklists of daily tasks that aren't necessarily meant to be scheduled like those you'd normally put on your calendar. It's there for your shopping lists, to-do lists, home improvement lists, and other general tasks. When you check off a task, it is removed from its current list and placed in the Completed list.

You can opt to save the tasks you create in the Reminders app to iCloud, just as you can with Notes. (If you have other compatible calendars, you can save reminders there.) From there, you can sync your reminders to other iDevices or simply use iCloud as a place to back them up. (At the present time, you can't sync reminders with iTunes to a computer.) Unlike with Notes, though, when you visit www.iCloud.com from a computer, you'll see your tasks in the Calendar section. You won't see your notes.

TIP

You enable iCloud for Reminders in the same place you configure other iCloud options by selecting **Settings | iCloud**.

Create a Reminder

Almost all views in the Reminders app offer the plus sign (+) button. You tap this button to add a reminder, and the reminder is created in whatever list is selected in the left pane. Nothing much happens when you do this, except the cursor appears at the bottom of your current list of reminders for the list you're in. You type (or dictate) the name of the task and tap RETURN on the virtual keyboard (or tap the microphone icon) to add it. It's really simple! See Figure 8-8.

If you decide to add data to the task later, tap the task in the list. From there you can change the task's name, set a reminder, repeat the task, set a priority, or add notes (under Show More). The way you do this is similar to what you've learned already when configuring events in Calendar: you tap and make choices, or tap and type. If you want to be reminded, though, you must tap **Remind Me**, and then enable **On A Day**. The Reminders app assumes you want to be reminded today, but you can change the date by tapping it.

Figure 8-8: **Add the task title first; then add the particulars later.**

Figure 8-9: *Notifications, such as those you set in the Reminders app, can be viewed from the Notification bar.*

Manage Reminders

You can view your tasks by opening the Reminders app, but you can also view tasks by dragging downward from the top of the iPad's interface on any screen. From the resulting list you can see your reminders, events stored on your Calendar, and other notifications. You can tap any item here to access it from your iPad. See Figure 8-9. If you don't see your reminders there, turn on reminders by selecting **Settings | Notifications**.

There are two lists available in the Reminders app: the Completed list and the Reminders list. (You may see other entries for compatible e-mail addresses, like Yahoo!.) You access these lists when List is selected across the top. You can add your own lists, however, to organize the tasks you create.

To create a new list:

1. In the Reminders app, verify that you are in List view.
2. If you have additional calendars (Yahoo! is shown here), make sure to tap **Reminders** under iCloud to create a new iCloud list.

3. Tap **Edit**.
4. Tap **Create New List**.
5. Name the list and tap **Done**.
6. Repeat as desired. Tap **Done** again when finished.

QUICK**FACTS**

UNDERSTANDING REMINDERS AND iCLOUD

When you enable Reminders for iCloud, your reminders are stored there for safekeeping. You can also access them by navigating to www.icloud.com. Select **Settings | iCloud** to configure the setting.

If you have other iDevices and have opted to store your reminders in iCloud, and if you've enabled iCloud on those devices, the first time you open the Reminders app you will see all of the reminders you've created (but have yet to delete) on all of your iDevices. If there are too many, it's easy to delete reminders you no longer need; just tap the reminder you want to delete, and tap **Delete**. However, because reminders are stored in iCloud, it's important to understand that deleting a reminder on your iPad will also delete it on other devices.

Now, anytime you want to create a task for a specific list, simply tap the list first. To create a task in the list, tap the plus sign and type the task name. As you did before, if you want to edit a task, tap it.

Finally, you can configure settings for the Reminders app. Reminders settings are available in the Mail, Contacts, Calendars section of the Settings app. You get only two options: Sync and Default List. Sync determines how far back your reminders are synced. You can choose to sync reminders from two weeks to six months back, or to sync all reminders. The default value is a single month. Default List determines which list new reminders that you add outside of the Reminders app will go to. You probably won't use this feature until new apps become available to use it.

Chapter 9
Syncing, Backing Up, and Restoring

In this chapter you'll learn how to sync, back up, and restore your iPad. These are all important maintenance tasks. It's not something you do for fun, but it is what you do to keep your data secure and your iPad up to date.Here, you'll first learn how to perform syncing tasks using iTunes and your computer. This is very important, even if you use iCloud for certain sync tasks and purchase all of your media from Apple. After that, you'll learn what can be stored in iCloud and how syncing occurs there. Finally, you'll learn how to restore your iPad from the various backups—both those available in iTunes on your computer and the data stored in iCloud.

Before we get started, you should understand the basic terms we'll be using. Syncing is transferring data and media changes from one device to another and back again, thus keeping the data on both devices *in sync*. You can sync data from your iPad to your computer and back again, or from your iPad to iCloud and back again (or both). Syncing keeps your iPad's data up to date and on the same page, so to speak, with your computer and/or the data stored in iCloud.

Backing up is part of syncing, and is achieved each time you connect your iPad to your computer. These are complete backups and are a necessary part of maintaining your iPad. If you configure it, backups can be created in iCloud too. However, at your computer, you can encrypt (encode) your backups to further secure them, and back up your backups for even more peace of mind. You can restore everything from a single place if something goes wrong, too. That's why we'll spend so much time discussing syncing and backing up with iTunes and your computer here; you should back up your iPad to your computer on a regular basis, even if you use iCloud.

If you still aren't convinced you need iTunes, here are a few other notes about backing up with iTunes instead of iCloud. First, music and other media that you have not purchased through iTunes aren't backed up when you use iCloud, so you'll have to use iTunes to back up and restore that data anyway. Second, backups for TV show purchases are not available in all areas, and if you're in one of those areas, you will need to use iTunes for that as well. Finally, the bigger danger is that previous purchases will be unavailable for restoring if they are no longer available from iTunes, iBookstore, or the App Store.

Finally, restoring is returning your iPad to some earlier state or condition; this may involve only resetting the icons on the Home screen or resetting default settings or returning your iPad to the state it was in when you first purchased it. You can restore your iPad using a backup you've created too.

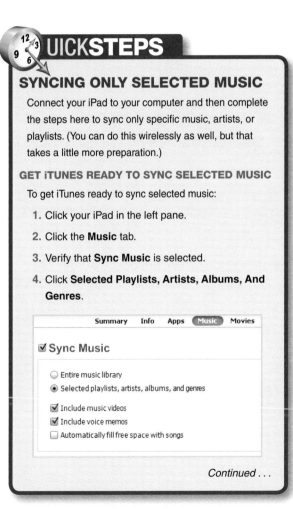

NOTE

Syncing using iTunes and iCloud is possible, and it's a good idea (especially if you use other iDevices); you just have to be sure you know what to sync and how.

QUICKSTEPS

SYNCING ONLY SELECTED MUSIC

Connect your iPad to your computer and then complete the steps here to sync only specific music, artists, or playlists. (You can do this wirelessly as well, but that takes a little more preparation.)

GET iTUNES READY TO SYNC SELECTED MUSIC

To get iTunes ready to sync selected music:

1. Click your iPad in the left pane.

2. Click the **Music** tab.

3. Verify that **Sync Music** is selected.

4. Click **Selected Playlists, Artists, Albums, And Genres**.

Summary Info Apps **Music** Movies

☑ **Sync Music**

○ Entire music library
● Selected playlists, artists, albums, and genres

☑ Include music videos
☑ Include voice memos
☐ Automatically fill free space with songs

Continued . . .

Configure Advanced Syncing with iTunes

You've already learned in various chapters in this book how to sync your iPad to your computer. However, more advanced syncing techniques are available that have not yet been introduced. For the most part, those techniques involve only syncing the data you want to sync so that you have exactly what you want on your iPad and nothing more. In addition to syncing only specific media, like photos, videos, and music, you can opt to sync calendar events, contacts, apps, and books, among other things.

Manage Music

You learned how to put music on your iPad by syncing with iTunes in Chapter 5. However, you may not have experimented with only syncing specific artists, albums, genres, playlists, and the like. Because you might have acquired quite a library of songs on your computer, it may be in your best interest to limit how much of that music syncs to your iPad.

Sync Contacts and Notes

You learned about the Contacts and Calendars apps in Chapter 8, and you learned a little about how to create calendars on your computer and sync them to your iPad. You didn't learn how to sync Contacts or Notes, however, two additional items available for syncing.

The way you sync your contacts depends on the e-mail program you use, the e-mail addresses you have configured, and other criteria, including whether or not you want to use iCloud for storing and backing up your contacts. As you can see in Figure 9-1, you may have several options when configuring syncing through iTunes. You'll have to decide which of your contact options you prefer.

The way you sync any notes you create also depends on the programs you have installed on your computer and whether or not you sync Notes with iCloud.

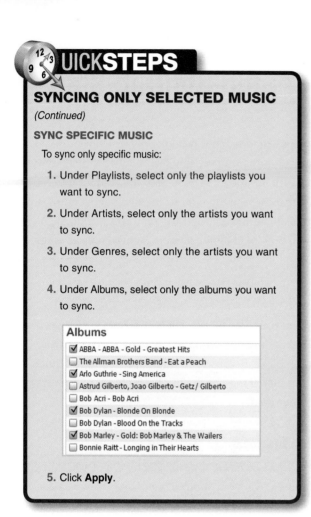

UICKSTEPS

SYNCING ONLY SELECTED MUSIC

(Continued)

SYNC SPECIFIC MUSIC

To sync only specific music:

1. Under Playlists, select only the playlists you want to sync.

2. Under Artists, select only the artists you want to sync.

3. Under Genres, select only the artists you want to sync.

4. Under Albums, select only the albums you want to sync.

Albums

☑ ABBA - ABBA - Gold - Greatest Hits
☐ The Allman Brothers Band - Eat a Peach
☑ Arlo Guthrie - Sing America
☐ Astrud Gilberto, Joao Gilberto - Getz / Gilberto
☐ Bob Acri - Bob Acri
☑ Bob Dylan - Blonde On Blonde
☐ Bob Dylan - Blood On the Tracks
☑ Bob Marley - Gold: Bob Marley & The Wailers
☐ Bonnie Raitt - Longing in Their Hearts

5. Click **Apply**.

Other

Bookmarks
Your bookmarks are being synced with your iPad over the air from iCloud.
Over-the-air sync settings can be changed on your iPad.

☑ Sync notes with | Outlook ⇕
Your notes are being synced over the air. Your notes will also sync directly with your device.

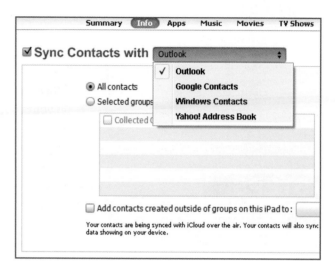

*Figure 9-1: **From the Info tab in iTunes, select which contacts you want to sync (if you do).***

Here it's okay to choose both; it's unlikely your notes will become muddled if you enable both (unless you use Notes in specific ways on multiple devices).

To sync contact data:

1. With your iPad connected to your computer, in iTunes, select your iPad in the left pane.

2. Click the **Info** tab.

3. Select **Sync Contacts With**; then:

   a. Click the arrow next to **With** (see Figure 9-1).

   b. Select the e-mail program you use on your computer.

   c. Select **All Contacts** or another option, if applicable.

4. Scroll down to Other, and select **Sync Notes With**; then:

   d. Click the arrow next to **With**.

   e. Select a compatible program you use on your computer.

5. Click **Apply**.

QUICKSTEPS

SYNCING ONLY SPECIFIC APPS

When you acquire apps and then sync your iPad with your computer, those apps are backed up to the computer along with the data you've amassed while using them. If you've backed up your iPad with iTunes, you can safely delete apps from your iPad when you tire of them and know that your app and its related data will be available from your computer if you want them again. You decide what to sync and not sync from the Apps tab in iTunes when your iPad is connected to your computer and selected.

To sync only specific apps:

1. Connect your iPad to your computer, and in iTunes, select the iPad in the left pane.

2. Click the **Apps** tab.

3. Select **Sync Apps**.

4. Select the apps you want to sync. (Note that you can sort the apps as well.)

5. Click **Apply**.

NOTE

You can access and redownload apps you've removed using your iPad. Look in the App Store under the Purchased tab.

Sync Mail Accounts

You might be tempted to simply select the option to sync your mail accounts and assume that your e-mail messages, contacts, passwords, and the like would be synced after clicking Apply. That's not what syncing mail accounts is all about, and none of that actually happens. When you opt to sync mail accounts, what you're doing is syncing your account *settings*. These are things like your Post Office Protocol 3 (POP3), Internet Message Access Protocol (IMAP), and Simple Message Transfer Protocol (SMTP) server names, your ports, and other technical data. If you set up your mail accounts in Chapter 3 and they're working properly, don't opt to sync these accounts. If you had problems in Chapter 3, you can try syncing your account settings here.

To sync mail account settings:

1. With your iPad connected to your computer, in iTunes, select your iPad in the left pane.

2. Click the **Info** tab.

3. Select **Sync Mail Accounts From**.

4. Select the e-mail program you use on your computer to obtain e-mail from the account (see Figure 9-2).

5. Click **Apply**.

Figure 9-2: **You can sync e-mail account settings, but only do this if you could not set up your mail accounts manually.**

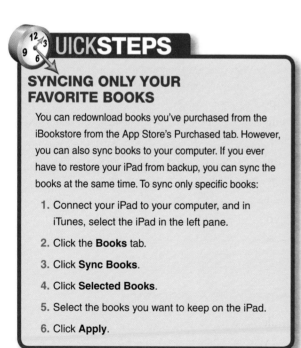

TIP

You can reposition the apps on your iPad from the Apps page in iTunes when the iPad is connected to your computer. You'll have access to all of your Home pages from the Apps page as well. Just click the page you want to configure to get started. Note you can click an app in iTunes to remove it, among other things.

QUICKSTEPS

SYNCING ONLY YOUR FAVORITE BOOKS

You can redownload books you've purchased from the iBookstore from the App Store's Purchased tab. However, you can also sync books to your computer. If you ever have to restore your iPad from backup, you can sync the books at the same time. To sync only specific books:

1. Connect your iPad to your computer, and in iTunes, select the iPad in the left pane.

2. Click the **Books** tab.

3. Click **Sync Books**.

4. Click **Selected Books**.

5. Select the books you want to keep on the iPad.

6. Click **Apply**.

Sync Books

If you've purchased books from the iBookstore and read them, you may want to move them off your iPad yet keep them in case you want to read them again. You can do this from the Books tab of iTunes. Figure 9-3 shows this tab.

You can back up even more data individually. From the Books tab you can choose what audiobooks to sync. From the Info tab, you can choose the calendars to sync. And from the Movies, TV Shows, Podcasts, and other tabs, you can

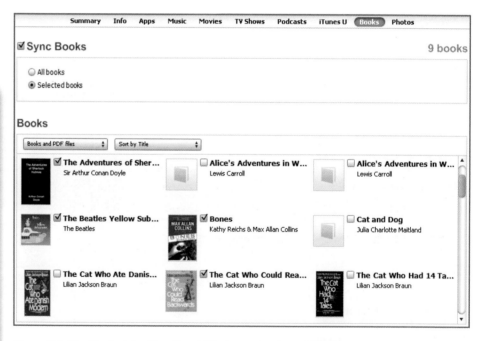

Figure 9-3: *The Books tab offers the ability to sync only specific books, such as those you've yet to read or want access to all the time.*

make even more choices. Make sure to work through all of the tabs before continuing here.

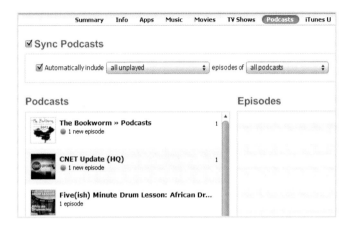

Back Up Your iPad

Backing up your iPad data is important, and you should back up your iPad regularly. We suggest you back up using iTunes and not iCloud. That's because iCloud only backs up your camera roll, accounts, documents, and settings. You have more data than that, including media you've obtained from places other than Apple. Another reason to back up to your computer is so that you can populate a new iPad quickly and easily if your iPad is lost, stolen, or broken and you replace it. You can also use your latest backup to restore an iPad that had to be reset to factory defaults because it wasn't functioning properly. (You can even back up your backups!)

Back Up to iTunes and Not to iCloud

As you know, we think you should back up your iPad using iTunes. Yes, you can rely on iCloud for backups if you don't have a computer. You can resync contacts, calendars, notes, and the like; and you can redownload apps from the App Store, media from iTunes, and even photos on your camera roll, your documents, and your settings, but this takes more time and effort, and won't include all of your data no matter how precise you are when you set your iCloud sync and backup options. It will also take quite a bit of time to restore this data individually. If you have a computer and you back up that computer regularly, use iTunes instead.

To choose to back up to your computer and not to iCloud:

1. From your iPad, tap **Settings** on the Home screen.

2. Tap **iCloud**.

3. Tap **Storage & Backup**.

4. Turn off iCloud Backup.

5. Connect your iPad to your computer, and from iTunes verify the option to back up using iTunes is enabled (see Figure 9-4).

From now on, when you connect your iPad to your computer, iTunes will perform a simple backup. This backup includes your apps, the settings you've configured, application data, and various other data that is directly related to the iPad.

You can also configure iTunes to wirelessly and automatically back up your iPad when certain conditions are met. However, you must first enable this in the iTunes from the Summary tab, under Options.

Version

| Check for Update | Your iPad software is up to date. iTunes will automatically check for an update again on 5/21/2012. |
| Restore | If you are experiencing problems with your iPad, you can restore its original settings by clicking Restore. |

Backup

○ Back up to iCloud
● Back up to this computer
    ☐ Encrypt local backup   Change Password...

Last backed up to this computer: 5/9/2012 12:34 PM

Figure 9-4: Opt to back up to your computer instead of iTunes.

Options

☑ Open iTunes when this iPad is connected
☑ Sync with this iPad over Wi-Fi
☐ Sync only checked songs and videos
☐ Prefer standard definition videos
☐ Convert higher bit rate songs to [128 kbps ▼] AAC
☐ Manually manage music and videos

Configure Universal Access...

TIP

When you use a password and encrypt your backups, make sure you write the password down and keep it in a safe place.

With that done, you can sync and back up wirelessly when the following conditions are met:

- Your iPad is plugged in to a wall outlet and it is powered on, although it can be asleep.
- iTunes is running on your computer, and the computer is awake.
- Your iPad and your computer are connected to your home Wi-Fi network.

You can manually create a backup by connecting your iPad to your computer anytime, provided connectivity options are met. To manually create a backup:

1. Connect your iPad to your computer.
2. Right-click your iPad in the sidebar of iTunes.
3. Click **Backup**.

Encrypt Your Backups

For extra security, you can set iTunes to encrypt your backups. When you encrypt your backups, you assign a password to them. You'll have to provide the password to restore the data later, should you need to. This will keep others from accessing your backup and keep the backup more secure.

To encrypt your backup:

1. Connect your iPad to your computer.
2. In iTunes, select your iPad in the left pane.
3. Click the **Summary** tab.
4. Select **Encrypt Local Backup**.
5. Type a password, type it again, and then click **Set Password**.

Back Up Your Backups

iPad backups, at least on PCs, are stored (and hidden away) in your User's folder. It's also likely that your music is stored in your Music folder, videos in the Videos folder, pictures in the Pictures folder, and so on. These are all subfolders of your User's folder. You can back up your iPad data as well as your personal data by backing up this personal folder. Macs perform and organize data similarly.

9

1 2 3 4 5 6 7 8 10

One way to back up your data is to use a backup program. Windows offers a program called Backup and Restore. The first time you run it, you'll be prompted to set it up. During the setup process, make sure that you back up your User's folder and, if available, create a system image. This will copy everything and save it to an external source, which will be a great help if something happens to the computer that holds your iPad backups and your iPad.

Use iCloud If You Don't Have a Computer

If you don't have a computer, you'll have to rely on iCloud alone. This is certainly doable and works for many people. As you know, you can redownload your purchased apps from the App Store, purchased media from the iTunes Store (see the image here), and even magazines and newspapers from the Newsstand Store.

You can also store personal data in iCloud. By selecting **Settings | iCloud** you can opt to store data from the following apps: Mail, Contacts, Calendars, Reminders, Bookmarks, and Notes. See Figure 9-5. You can also store photos you take using Photo Stream, and you can opt to save some additional types of documents and data.

From Storage & Backup, you can also manage your iCloud storage, buy more storage, and turn iCloud Backup on or off. The latter will automatically back up your camera roll, accounts, documents,

![iCloud settings screen showing Settings menu on left with Airplane Mode, Wi-Fi, Notifications, Location Services, Cellular Data, Brightness & Wallpaper, Picture Frame, General, iCloud, Mail Contacts Calendars, Twitter, FaceTime, Safari, Messages, Music, Video; and on right iCloud pane with Account joliballew@gmail.com, Mail ON, Contacts ON, Calendars ON, Reminders ON, Bookmarks ON, Notes ON, Photo Stream On, Documents & Data On, Find My iPad ON, Storage & Backup, Delete Account]

Figure 9-5: **You can use iCloud to back up some types of personal data.**

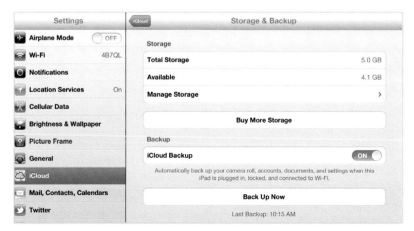

and settings when the iPad is plugged in, locked, and connected to Wi-Fi.

Use iCloud

To use iCloud, select **Settings | iCloud**. Turn on iCloud for the desired data. You've learned a lot about this throughout this book. In addition, to create limited backups using iCloud (if a computer is not available), enable iCloud Backup by selecting **Settings | iCloud | Storage & Backup**. (If you decide later to back up using iTunes and your computer, return here and change the setting to Off.)

From Storage & Backup you can also tap Manage Storage. From there you can see exactly what you're storing and how much space it takes up. Here is what is stored on my iPad, and you may see something similar. Note the options you can choose here: You can enable or disable online storage for various apps, including iBooks, iTunes U, and more.

Restore from the Cloud

If you don't have a backup available from iTunes at your computer and you need to restore an iPad that's been reset to factory defaults or you need to populate a new iPad with data from your Apple ID, you can, provided you have already been using iCloud for backup. It just takes a bit of effort. Here are a few things you can do:

- If your iPad is new or was reset to factory defaults, during setup, provide the Apple ID you've always used.

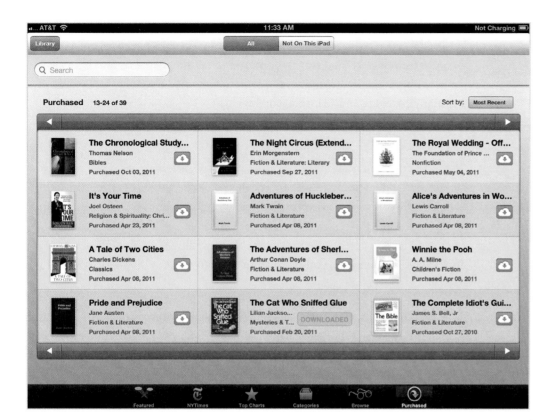

- If prompted to use iCloud, choose **Yes**.

- If prompted to restore from an iCloud backup and one is available, choose to do so.

- Once your iPad is ready and the Home screen available, visit iTunes. Click the **Purchased** tab and redownload the desired data. Repeat with the App Store.

- Select **Settings | iCloud**, and turn on iCloud for the desired data.

- Sign in to Game Center and follow any prompts to provide your ID.

- Open Newsstand and reacquire magazines and newspapers.

- Download and open iBooks, tap **Store**, and from the Purchased tab, redownload the desired books.

- Use third-party apps like Audible to reacquire purchased media.

Update Your iPad

Once in a while, Apple makes an update available for your iPad. You'll get an alert when an update is available, and you should always opt to install the update. Make sure your iPad is charged or plugged in before you start, though, and that you have a little time to let your iPad perform the task. When you're ready, you can then either tap the alert window to access the update information, or you can select **Settings | General | Software Update**. You can install the update wirelessly. Once the update is installed, you'll see that the iPad is up to date, as shown in Figure 9-6.

Figure 9-6: **Your iPad's software is very likely up to date.**

TIP

You also can check for updates to iTunes from the Help menu (Check For Updates).

QUICKSTEPS

TAKING ACTION WHEN YOUR iPAD IS "FROZEN"

If your iPad isn't responding and seems to be "frozen," you can try several things before you opt to reset or restore from a backup:

- If your screen won't rotate, verify that the screen rotation lock is not engaged. Likewise, if there's no sound, verify that the silent switch, located just above the volume rocker, has not been enabled and that the volume rocker is set to produce sound. If you'd rather, use any method to access the Multitasking bar, and then flick from left to right on that bar to access the screen rotation and volume controls.

- If an application seems to be the cause of the iPad's unresponsiveness, press and hold the **Sleep/Wake** button. When the red slider appears, let go of the **Sleep/Wake** button and then press and hold the **Home** button. This should close the current application. Your iPad may be just fine after that. Sometimes third-party apps are "buggy" and cause the iPad to freeze up. If you deem this to be the case, it's best to uninstall or delete the app.

- You can also close any app manually that appears in the Multitasking bar. To do this, show the Multitasking bar and then tap and hold any app until they all start to jiggle. Then, tap the red minus sign (–) available on the app to close it.

Continued . . .

Restore or Reset Your iPad

You can restore your iPad from a backup if something happens to it or if you have to buy a new iPad. You can reset an existing iPad's settings to the default settings or prepare an iPad for a new owner.

Restore from a Backup

If you've created a backup using iTunes, you have a copy of your settings, application data, your iPad's operating system, and various other pertinent data. And if you've synced your iPad with your computer, you have a backup of all of your media too. You can restore from these two backups should you ever need to. You can restore the data to your existing iPad, or, if the iPad was lost, stolen, or damaged, you can restore to a new iPad.

To restore your iPad from a backup:

1. At the computer where you manage your iPad, connect to the Internet.

2. Connect your iPad to the computer.

3. In iTunes, right-click on a PC or **CTRL**+click on a Mac on the iPad in the sidebar, and then choose **Restore From Backup** from the context menu that appears.

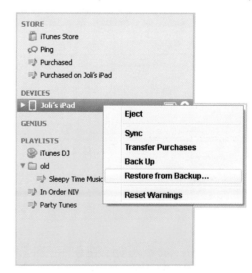

TAKING ACTION WHEN YOUR iPAD IS "FROZEN" *(Continued)*

- If the battery is low on power, charge the iPad by connecting it to a wall outlet using the power adapter. A low battery shouldn't cause the iPad to freeze up, but it might "go to sleep" while you're trying to use it.

- If the previous options don't work or are not the issue, you'll need to turn off the iPad and turn it back on. Press and hold the **Sleep/Wake** button, and when the red slider appears, drag the slider to turn off the iPad. Then press and hold the **Sleep/Wake** button again to turn the iPad back on.

- As a last resort, reset the iPad. Resetting won't cause data loss if you choose the right option; it's like rebooting a computer. Press and hold the **Sleep/Wake** button and the **Home** button simultaneously for ten seconds. When the Apple logo appears, let go. The iPad will reset.

TIP

You can show the Multitasking bar using a four-finger swipe upward or by double-pressing the Home button. Close it by touching outside of it or by pressing the Home button.

4. Choose the backup that you want to restore from, and then click **Restore**. Use the drop-down menu to review your options. If the backup is encrypted, you'll need to enter your password.

5. Your iPad will restart. Leave it connected until it's finished; it could take some time.

Restore to Factory Settings

The only time you'll want to restore your iPad to factory settings is if you want to sell it, give it away, or completely start fresh. Restoring to factory settings will erase everything on your iPad, including your personal data, apps, books, and any other data you've acquired (although it won't erase this data from your computer, should you be interested in, say, upgrading to a new iPad sometime in the future). Your settings, preferences, preferred networks, and everything else will be reset to the defaults. Restoring to factory settings makes the iPad look and act like it did the day you brought it home.

If you have a computer and iTunes, you can connect your iPad to your computer, and from the Summary tab in iTunes, click **Restore**. This will restore your iPad to factory settings.

You can also restore directly from your iPad:

1. From your iPad, tap **Settings**.
2. Tap **General**.
3. Tap **Reset**.
4. Tap **Erase All Content And Settings**.
5. Once the restore is complete, disconnect your iPad and do not sync it again if you want to give it away or sell it. (You can sync it to restore from a backup though.)

QUICKSTEPS

RESETTING YOUR HOME SCREEN LAYOUT

When you reset your Home screen layout, the default Home screen will be returned to its native configuration. Apps that are not supposed to be on the Home screen will be moved to other screens.

To reset your Home screen layout:

1. Tap **Settings**.

2. Tap **General**.

3. Scroll down and tap **Reset**.

4. Tap **Reset Home Screen Layout**.

5. If applicable, input your passcode.

6. Tap **Reset** to apply or **Cancel** to quit.

Reset Your iPad

Using your iPad, you can reset the following:

- **Reset All Settings**   This will reset all settings but will not delete any media or personal data.

- **Erase All Content And Settings**   Outlined in the previous section, this option returns the iPad to factory defaults and erases all personal data, apps, media, and personal settings.

- **Reset Network Settings**   This will delete all network settings, returning them to factory defaults.

- **Reset Keyboard Dictionary**   This will delete all custom words you have typed on the keyboard, returning the keyboard dictionary to factory defaults.

- **Reset Home Screen Layout**   This will reset your Home screen layout to factory defaults.

- **Reset Location Warnings**   This will reset your location warnings to factory defaults.

How to...

Chapter 10
Exploring Settings

Throughout this book, you've configured some settings for apps on your iPad. In Chapter 1 you used the Settings app to apply a passcode lock to protect your iPad; in Chapter 2 you enabled Wi-Fi and cellular data features so you could get online; in Chapter 3 you explored some of the available Mail settings, including how to use gestures to manage your mail—you get the idea. However, it's important to explore all of the options in the Settings app so that you can return here as needed and make configuration changes.

This chapter explains what's available in the Settings app. Configuring settings is generally a straightforward process, once you know where to find what you need.

Explore Settings

The Settings app enables you to customize your iPad's apps and set preferences. This is where you'll go to change your wallpaper, configure settings for Safari, and configure preferences for Picture Frame, among other things. There's a wide range of settings to choose from and lots of preferences you can set. You can configure preferences and settings in the following categories:

- Airplane Mode
- Wi-Fi
- Notifications
- Location Services
- Cellular Data (only available on iPads with cellular features)
- Brightness and Wallpaper
- Picture Frame
- General
- iCloud
- Mail, Contacts, Calendars
- Twitter
- FaceTime
- Safari
- Messages
- Music
- Video
- Photos
- Notes
- Store

Although we've introduced some of these settings in this book, this chapter outlines what you can do within each category of settings. The chapter is organized by what you can *do;* it is not simply a list of settings and how to enable or disable them (which was covered throughout this book).

NOTE

Each time you change a setting in the Settings app, the change is applied immediately. You do not have to tap **Save**, for example.

Use Airplane Mode

When you are on an airplane, you'll often be advised when you can use "approved devices." The iPad is one of those approved devices, provided you disable the wireless features. You may want to enable Airplane Mode to increase battery life when you know you won't be connecting to any networks as well. For more information about networks, see Chapter 2.

To enable Airplane Mode:

1. Tap **Settings**.

2. Tap the slider next to Airplane Mode (moving it from Off to On).

3. Tap again to turn off Airplane Mode. You can see this option in Figure 10-1 in the next section.

Enable, Disable, and Manage Wi-Fi

You configure Wi-Fi settings to state how the iPad should use local Wi-Fi networks to connect to the Internet. You'll want to leave Wi-Fi enabled when you know you'll be accessing the Internet from your home network or a wireless hotspot. If no Wi-Fi networks are available, or if you turn Wi-Fi off, the iPad will connect to the Internet over your cellular data network (on iPad Wi-Fi + cellular models only), if it's available, and if you subscribe to a cellular data service. For more information about networks, see Chapter 2.

Wi-Fi options include the ability to:

- **Turn Wi-Fi on or off**   See Figure 10-1.

- **Join a Wi-Fi network**   You first select a network from the list, and then enter a password if necessary.

- **Set iPad to ask if you want to join available networks**   This will notify you when networks are available (or not).

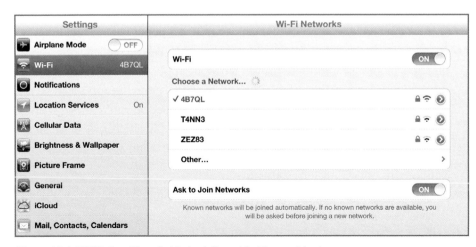

*Figure 10-1: **Wi-Fi should probably be left enabled in most instances.***

TIP

To save on data usage, disable unnecessary alerts from Notifications.

QUICKSTEPS

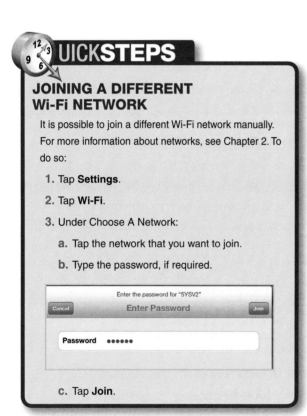

JOINING A DIFFERENT Wi-Fi NETWORK

It is possible to join a different Wi-Fi network manually. For more information about networks, see Chapter 2. To do so:

1. Tap **Settings**.

2. Tap **Wi-Fi**.

3. Under Choose A Network:

   a. Tap the network that you want to join.

   b. Type the password, if required.

   c. Tap **Join**.

- **Forget a network so iPad doesn't join it automatically** You want to "forget" networks you know you'll never use, because your iPad works through all of the networks when looking for one. This uses battery power and takes time. It's best to keep the list short and only filled with networks you recognize. To do this, tap the blue arrow next to a network you've connected to before, and then tap **Forget This Network**.

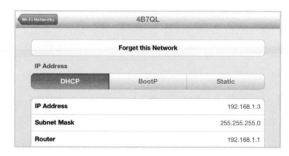

- **Join a closed Wi-Fi network** To join a Wi-Fi network that isn't shown in the list of networks, tap **Other** and then enter the network name and other required information, such as a password.

- **Adjust settings to connect to a Wi-Fi network** Change settings for your current Wi-Fi network. Tap the blue arrow beside the network name to access the settings.

Manage Notifications

When you configure the Game Center, install the Twitter app, enable Messages, install certain third-party apps, or perform similar tasks, you'll be asked to allow the app to send notifications to your iPad automatically. These notifications can include badges, alerts, and sounds. When enabled, apps can alert you about new information, even when the application isn't running. Most notifications play a sound, offer text, or place a number on the app's icon on the Home screen. You may want notifications to be enabled so you'll know when it's your turn to play a game, when you're mentioned in a tweet, or when an event occurs in Calendar. For more information about using apps, see Chapter 6.

Notifications options include the ability to:

- **State in what order apps appear in the Notification Center** They can be sorted manually or by the time they arrived.

- **Turn some or all notifications on or off** This enables you to turn off notifications for a specific app. See Figure 10-2.

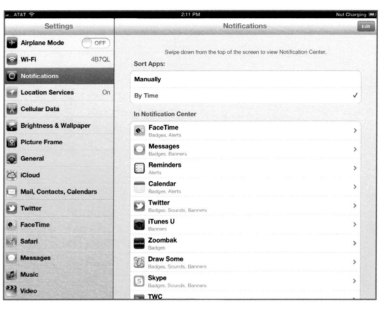

Figure 10-2: Apps that offer notifications will appear in the Notifications section of Settings.

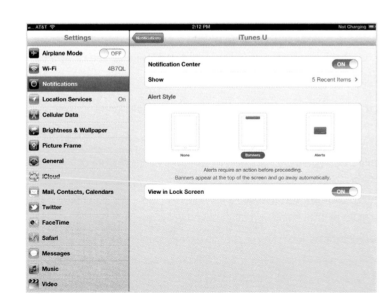

To turn off notifications for any app:

1. Tap **Settings**.

2. Tap **Notifications**.

3. Tap the arrow associated with the app you want to change.

4. In the resulting page, opt to turn off the notifications you do not want sent to you. This might include Sounds, Alerts, or Badges, for instance.

Configure Location Services

Location Services is what enables an app, say Maps, the Camera, and other apps (including third-party apps), to determine your approximate location. You may want to disable this to maintain your privacy. However, most apps that want information regarding your location want it to make your experience with the app more valuable. For instance, when Location Services for Maps is enabled, you can tap the Location icon to let Maps figure out where you are, perhaps to use as a starting point for directions you'd like to acquire. Third-party apps, such as Bing for iPad, use your location to offer information about the weather and local businesses, among other things.

Location Services includes the ability to

- **Turn Location Services on or off** This enables or disables Location Services for all apps.

- **Turn Location Services on or off for specific apps** Turn on or off Location Services for only the apps you want.

Enable, Disable, and Manage Cellular Data

Cellular Data settings are available only on the iPad Wi-Fi + 4G model (in some countries this is called the Wi-Fi + Cellular model). They enable you to change settings related to your current cellular data network and turn cellular data and/or roaming on or off. For more information about networks, see Chapter 2.

Cellular Data options include the ability to:

- **Turn the cellular data network connection on or off** You may want to turn off cellular network access when you know you'll be away from Wi-Fi networks but also know you won't need Internet access.

- **Enable or disable LTE** When enabled, data loads faster, but uses more of your iPad's battery power.

- **Turn data roaming on or off** Data roaming may cost extra if you're out of the country. It's best to leave this off until you fully understand your plan.

- **View your account information** See or change your account information.

- **Add a SIM PIN** You can add a personal identification number (PIN) to lock your micro-SIM card. If your iPad is stolen, a thief could possibly pull out the SIM card and obtain data from it.

TIP

To avoid unwanted charges, turn off data roaming.

TIP

Reduce brightness to increase battery life.

Change Brightness and Wallpaper

Use Brightness settings to adjust the screen brightness and Wallpaper settings to personalize your iPad's Home screen wallpaper and the picture you see when you unlock your iPad. For more information about personalizing your iPad with wallpaper, see Chapter 1.

Brightness and Wallpaper options include the ability to:

- **Adjust the screen brightness** You do this using a slider.
- **Set whether iPad adjusts screen brightness automatically** Enable or disable Auto-Brightness. When Auto-Brightness is enabled, your iPad will adjust the brightness automatically using the built-in ambient light sensor.
- **Set wallpaper** Select a wallpaper for the Lock screen, Home screen, or both. Figure 10-3 shows the available wallpapers from Apple, but you can choose from your own photos if you'd rather.

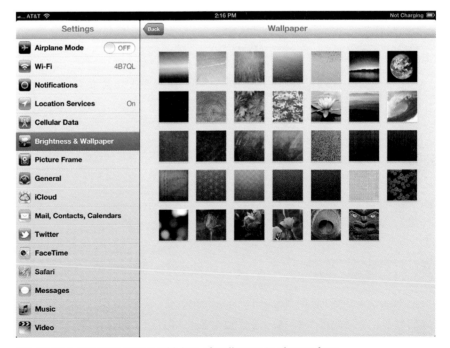

Figure 10-3: ***The iPad comes with lots of wallpaper to choose from.***

10

Configure Picture Frame

You can use your iPad as a digital picture frame. You can enhance this by also incorporating the optional dock to hold the frame in place on a mantle or table, although any compatible stand will work. You can also use the Smart Cover, if you have one. Picture Frame mode lets you also apply transitions in between photos and choose what photos to display. You can even zoom in on faces and shuffle photos when playing them. For more information about sharing pictures, see Chapter 4.

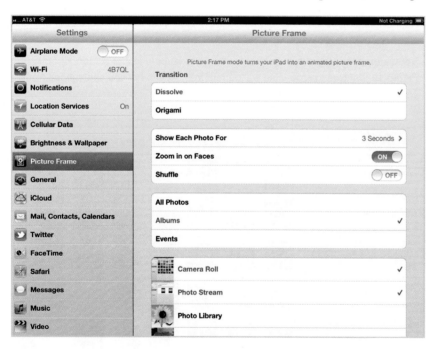

Picture Frame options include the ability to:

- **Select a transition** Choose the type of transition to use between photos.

- **Show a picture for a specific time** Specify how long a picture should remain on the screen until it moves to the next one.

- **Zoom in on faces during a Picture Frame show** This option only works when Dissolve is selected as the transition.

- **Shuffle** Randomizes the order in which photos are displayed.

- **Choose what pictures to show** Select a folder or photos to use when Picture Frame is playing, or choose all photos.

Change General Settings

General settings include those related to the date and time, security, network, and other things that affect every part of your iPad. This is also where you can find information about your iPad, or reset your iPad to its original state. The General settings offer subcategories, that, when selected, offer even more options. Listed next are the subcategories and what they include.

TIP

To enhance battery life, turn off Bluetooth when you aren't using it.

The General settings contain more options than any other feature in the Settings app. To use this:

1. Tap **Settings** on the Home screen.

2. Tap **General**.

3. Use your finger to scroll down so you can see every option.

4. If an option has an arrow by it, there are suboptions available (see Figure 10-4). Tap any arrow to explore.

5. Tap the **Back** button or tap **General** to return to the previous screen.

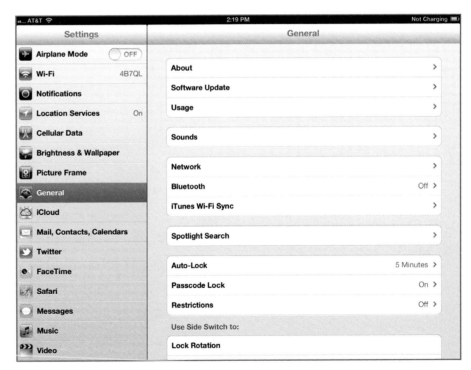

Figure 10-4: If you have a Smart Cover, you'll see an additional option from the General setting.

![NOTE]

What you see from the General category will look different from what you see here if you have a Smart Cover.

Name	Joli's iPad >
Network	AT&T
Songs	29
Videos	4
Photos	1,115
Applications	45
Capacity	13.3 GB
Available	3.6 GB
Version	5.1.1 (9B206)
Carrier	AT&T 12.0

ABOUT

Click About to get information about your iPad, including but not limited to, total storage capacity; available space; number of songs, videos, and photos; serial number; and software version.

SOFTWARE UPDATE

Tap the Software Update option to have your iPad check for updates or to install new updates.

USAGE

Click the Usage category to obtain information about what kinds of data you store on your iPad, how much data you have stored in iCloud (if applicable), and the amount of cellular data you've sent and received, among other things. For more information about using cellular networks, refer to Chapter 2.

Usage options include the ability to:

- **Manage onboard storage**   View how much of your iPad's storage is being used and by what type of data. You may find that videos are taking up quite a bit of storage space, for instance.

- **Manage iCloud storage**   View information about your iCloud storage, including total storage, how much is available, and how to manage it. You can access these options from the iCloud setting too.

- **Show battery percentage**   Display the percentage of battery charge next to the battery icon on the Home screen.

- **Review cellular usage**   View the amount of data sent and received over the cellular data network (on iPad Wi-Fi + 4G only) since the last time you reset your usage statistics. You can also reset your statistics here.

SOUNDS

Click Sounds to make changes to settings related to sounds. For more information about personalizing your iPad, see Chapter 1.

Sounds options include the ability to:

- **Adjust the ringer and alerts volume**
- **Set alert and effects sounds**   Turn specific sounds on or off. You can enable or disable sounds for the following:
  - Ringtones
  - Texts
  - Incoming e-mail messages
  - Sent e-mail messages
  - Tweets
  - Alerts for events
  - Alerts for reminders
  - Locking the iPad
  - Typing using the keyboard

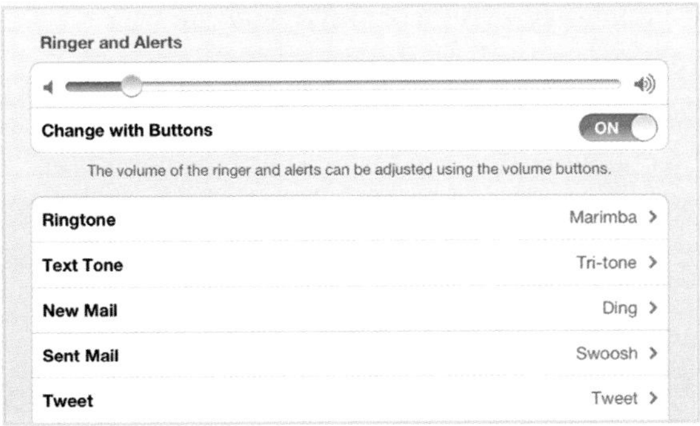

To make these changes:

1. In the Settings app, tap **General**.

2. Tap the arrow next to **Sounds**.

3. Tap the arrow next to **Ringtone** to change it, and then:
   a. Tap a new ringtone from the list.
   b. Tap **Sounds** (the Back button).
   c. Repeat as desired for other sounds.

4. Tap the **On** button on any other line shown under Ringtone to turn that sound off.

NETWORK

Network settings enable you to access and change settings related to the various networks you use, including Wi-Fi and virtual private networks (VPNs). VPNs offer secure connections to networks using the Internet. For more information about networks, see Chapter 2.

Ringer and Alerts

◀ ────○──────────────── ◀))

Change with Buttons　　　　　　　　ON

The volume of the ringer and alerts can be adjusted using the volume buttons.

Ringtone	Marimba >
Text Tone	Tri-tone >
New Mail	Ding >
Sent Mail	Swoosh >
Tweet	Tweet >

QUICKSTEPS

CONNECTING A BLUETOOTH DEVICE

A compatible Bluetooth device is a wireless device you can use with your iPad, such as a wireless headset, wireless speakers, or wireless keyboard. You must "pair" the device with your iPad. Pairing allows the device and the iPad to agree on a Bluetooth frequency so that they can communicate effectively without "crossing signals" with any other Bluetooth devices you may have installed.

To connect a Bluetooth device:

1. Turn on your new Bluetooth device, insert batteries, or perform any other step to power on the device.

2. Follow the directions for the device to make it discoverable. This may include pressing a "connect" button.

3. Locate and tap the **Settings** icon on the Home screen.

4. Tap **General**.

5. Tap **Bluetooth** and move the slider to **On**.

6. Wait while the iPad searches for Bluetooth devices.

7. When it finds the device, type the device's passkey or PIN as prompted. The device will connect. (If you have several available Bluetooth devices, you'll need to tap the name of the correct device first.)

8. To turn off Bluetooth, again tap **Settings**, then tap **General**, tap **Bluetooth**, and move the virtual switch to the **Off** position.

Network options include the ability to

- **Add a new VPN configuration**   You'll have to drill down into VPN settings to access this command.

- **Change a VPN configuration**

- **Turn VPN on or off**

- **Delete a VPN configuration**

- **Access Wi-Fi settings**   These are the Wi-Fi settings detailed earlier.

BLUETOOTH

Your iPad can connect to Bluetooth devices like headphones and keyboards. Bluetooth devices allow you to listen or type without wires (among other things). There are three options for Bluetooth:

- **Turn Bluetooth on or off**

- **Search for Bluetooth devices**   Watch while your iPad searches for Bluetooth devices once Bluetooth is enabled.

- **Connect to a Bluetooth device**   Pair your iPad with a Bluetooth device in range.

iTUNES Wi-Fi SYNC

When this option is enabled via iTunes and your computer, you can automatically force a sync here if all conditions for connectivity are met. The conditions include that the iPad must be plugged into a wall outlet, the iPad must be connected to your Wi-Fi network (the one that also has the computer you sync with on it), and the computer must be turned on with iTunes running.

SPOTLIGHT SEARCH

When you search from the Spotlight Search screen, the iPad searches through the data on it to find what you need. You can state which data Spotlight Search should consider. You can choose to enable or disable many types of data. You can also drag any item to the top of the list or the bottom, to have it searched first or last, or in any

Settings		General	Spotlight Search
Airplane Mode	OFF	✓ Contacts	
Wi-Fi	4B7QL	✓ Applications	
Notifications		✓ Music	
Location Services	On	✓ Podcasts	
Cellular Data		✓ Videos	
Brightness & Wallpaper		✓ Audiobooks	
Picture Frame		✓ Notes	
General		✓ Events	
iCloud		✓ Mail	
Mail, Contacts, Calendars		✓ Reminders	
Twitter		✓ Messages	

order desired. The only option here is to tell Spotlight Search what data to look through.

AUTO-LOCK

Here you can set how many minutes of idle time should pass before the iPad locks itself.

PASSCODE LOCK

You can secure your iPad by requiring a passcode lock. When you enable this feature, each time you unlock your iPad, you have to provide this code. This keeps it safe from unauthorized users. To enable Auto-Lock and Passcode Lock, see Chapter 1.

Passcode Lock options include the ability to:

- **Turn Passcode Lock on or off**
- **Set or change a passcode**   Enter a four-digit passcode.
- **Set how long before your passcode is required**   Set how long the iPad should be idle before you need to enter a passcode to unlock it.
- **Change from a simple passcode**   Stop using a four-digit passcode and change to a code you create from letters, numbers, and other typed characters.
- **Picture Frame**   When using a passcode lock with this option set to On, you'll be able to start a Picture Frame slideshow from the Lock screen without entering the passcode. When using a passcode lock with this option set to Off, you won't be able to start Picture Frame at all, because the Picture Frame icon won't appear on the Lock screen.
- **Erase data after 10 failed passcode attempts**   If you turn on this feature, after 10 failed passcode attempts the iPad erases all your information and media. See Figure 10-5.

NOTE

You will have an option that falls between Passcode Lock and Restrictions called iPad Cover Lock/Unlock if you have a Smart Cover. You can turn it on or off. When turned on, closing the cover will automatically cause the iPad to sleep. Opening the cover will automatically wake the iPad and skip the "slide to open" lock screen and go straight to the passcode entry screen (if you're using one), or to the last thing you were doing when you aren't using the passcode lock.

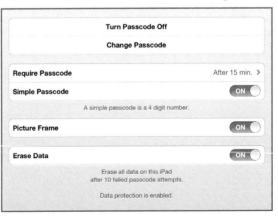

Turn Passcode Off	
Change Passcode	
Require Passcode	After 15 min. >
Simple Passcode	ON
A simple passcode is a 4 digit number.	
Picture Frame	ON
Erase Data	ON
Erase all data on this iPad after 10 failed passcode attempts.	
Data protection is enabled.	

Figure 10-5: It's best to set a passcode, even a simple one, and require it after a short period of time.

RESTRICTIONS

Restrictions on the iPad are kind of like parental controls on other devices. You can set restrictions for music, movies, and similar content on the iPad, as well as a few other applications like YouTube or iTunes. When you configure Restrictions, create a different passcode from the one you use to unlock your iPad for extra security. (Your children may know your passcode lock.)

Restrictions options include the ability to:

- **Enable or disable restrictions**   You'll have to create and enter a four-digit passcode to enable or disable restrictions.

- **Set application restrictions**   Set restrictions on individual apps, including Safari, YouTube, Camera, FaceTime, iTunes, and Ping; installing apps; and deleting apps. You can also disable restrictions for dictation and having dictation type explicit language. You can also allow or disallow changes to location and accounts.

- **Set allowed content**   Set restrictions on the type of content that can be played with regard to ratings. These include music and podcasts, movies, TV shows, apps, and in-app purchases. If you restrict in-app purchases, make sure to set Require Password to Immediately. You can also restrict Game Center's multiplayer games as well as the ability to add friends.

SIDE SWITCH

Here you configure what you want the side switch to do. It can be a lock rotation or it can mute the iPad.

MULTITASKING GESTURES

This gives you the ability to enable or disable multitasking gestures. When enabled, you can use various four- and five-finger techniques to access the Home screen, reveal the Multitasking bar, and move between running apps, among other things.

DATE AND TIME

Settings are available to personalize the date and time information on your iPad.

These options include the ability to:

- **Set whether iPad shows 24-hour time or 12-hour time**
- **Set automatically**   With this feature activated, the iPad sets the time automatically. If it is turned off, you can manually set a time zone as well as a date and time.
- **Choose a time zone**

KEYBOARD

You can change various settings for the keyboard and set preferences for how you type. For instance, you can turn the Auto-Capitalization feature on or off if you'd rather not have the iPad automatically capitalize the beginning of sentences.

Keyboard options include the ability to:

- **Turn Auto-Capitalization on or off**
- **Turn Auto-Correction on or off**
- **Check spelling**
- **Set whether the Caps Lock feature is enabled**   Enabling this setting lets you double-tap the **SHIFT** key to engage Caps Lock mode. If disabled, a double-tap does not engage Caps Lock mode.
- **Turn the "." shortcut on or off**   The "." shortcut lets you double-tap the **SPACEBAR** to enter a period followed by a space when you're typing.
- **Set up international keyboards**   Add and configure keyboards for multiple languages.
- **Turn the split keyboard on or off**
- **Enable or disable dictation from the keyboard**
- **Create typing shortcuts**   To create shortcuts you can use while typing. One already exists: "omw," which, once typed, will result in the words "On my way!" appearing on the screen.

INTERNATIONAL

Your iPad comes with various international settings. With these, you can set the language for the iPad, turn keyboards for different languages on or off, and configure similar preferences for your preferred language.

International options include the ability to:

- **Set the language for the iPad**
- **Set up international keyboards**
- **Set date, time, and telephone number formats for your specific region**
- **Set calendar**   You can currently choose from Gregorian, Japanese, and Buddhist.

ACCESSIBILITY

Accessibility options make it easier for a person with a visual, physical, or hearing disability to use the iPad.

Accessibility options include the ability to:

- **Have what's on your iPad's screen read to you using VoiceOver**
- **Zoom in on your iPad's screen**
- **Use large text**   This makes text larger in some of the default apps.
- **Use a high-contrast screen**   This uses the white-on-black screen mode.
- **Have the iPad speak text selections**
- **Speak auto-text**   Have the iPad speak auto-corrections and auto-capitalizations to you.
- **Use mono audio**   Combine stereo audio channels so that identical sound is heard in both.
- **Enable AssistiveTouch**   This allows you to use the iPad with an adaptive accessory.
- **Triple-click Home**   This allows you to triple-click the Home button to toggle some accessibility features.

RESET THE IPAD

You will change the default values for various settings on your iPad as you use it. You'll likely reorder the Home screen, add words to the dictionary while typing, or change network settings. You can reset these by resetting specific apps on your iPad. You can also reset your iPad and delete everything on it, restoring it to factory settings.

TIP

Before you sell, trade, give, or donate your iPad, erase all content and settings.

Resetting iPad options include the ability to:

- **Reset all settings**   This only applies to settings on the iPad, not your data (like contacts, calendars, and media).
- **Erase all content and settings**   This completely resets your iPad and deletes all of the data on it.
- **Reset network settings**
- **Reset the keyboard dictionary**
- **Reset the Home screen layout**
- **Reset the location warnings**

Configure iCloud

iCloud is a place to store certain data on Internet servers. You can also sync that data from iCloud to other iDevices. From the iCloud options detailed here, you can configure exactly what you want to sync with iCloud servers, from mail to contacts to notes and more. You'll also find an iCloud option for mail in the Mail, Contacts, Calendars section, detailed next. In both areas, you can enable Find My iPad too, which will help you locate your iPad if it goes missing.

- **Manage an iCloud account**   Choose an iCloud account to manage.
- **Turn on or off specific apps for iCloud use**   Choose which apps you want to sync to iCloud.
- **Enable Find My iPad**   Set up Find My iPad so you can locate it should you lose it.
- **Manage Storage & Backup**   See your total iCloud storage, what's available, and manage that storage. You can also buy more storage and turn iCloud backups on and off. You can also back up manually by tapping Back Up Now.

Set Defaults for Mail, Contacts, Calendars

You'll use the Mail, Contacts, Calendars settings to set up e-mail accounts and manage them. You can also customize preferences for these accounts and related features, including Contacts and Calendar. For more information about setting up Mail, see Chapter 3. For more information about the Contacts and Calendar apps, refer to Chapter 8.

Figure 10-6: *As with other apps, arrows indicate that several options are available for a setting.*

To use the Mail, Contacts, Calendars options:

1. In the Settings app, tap **Mail, Contacts, Calendars**.
2. Scroll through the options in the right pane to explore them.
3. If an option has an arrow by it, tap the arrow to access the options.
4. Tap any option to change it. Figure 10-6 shows the Mail, Contacts, Calendars screen.

ACCOUNTS

This is where you configure the e-mail accounts and calendar subscriptions on your iPad. You can change your account settings, stop using an account, or even delete an account.

Account options include the ability to:

● **Manage your iCloud account**   Choose what you'd like to sync with iCloud.
● **Change an account's settings**   Choose an existing account and make changes to it.
● **Stop using an account**   Disable an account.
● **Adjust advanced settings**   For e-mail accounts, configure options such as mailbox behaviors and settings for incoming messages.
● **Delete an account from iPad**   This deletes an account completely. If you want to use the account again, you'll have to reenter it. If you aren't sure, disable the account instead.

FETCH NEW DATA

Fetch and Push are two ways to obtain your e-mail. Push is a technology that allows Internet servers to send information to your iPad as soon as the message is received by your e-mail provider on their e-mail servers. Some e-mail servers will push e-mail to you, while others won't. Be aware that using Push will use battery power to obtain updates and transfer data, and can minimize battery life. Transfers while connected via cellular networks are counted toward your monthly data usage as well. This isn't a problem if you have a generous data plan, but it can be if you have a limited plan.

For e-mail accounts that are not push compatible, no e-mail will arrive at your Inbox in Mail until you open Mail and access it. At that time, Mail will check for e-mail and obtain it from your e-mail servers. If this is inconvenient and you'd rather have Mail check for e-mail automatically, even when you aren't using it, you can configure your iPad to fetch your e-mail on a schedule, such as every 15, 30, or 60 minutes. You can also set Fetch settings to Manually so that no fetch occurs by default. As with Push, Fetch will drain your battery more quickly on than off. To maximize battery life, fetch less often or fetch manually. Fetch also kicks in for Push e-mail accounts if Push is turned off, so if you're watching your data usage, you may need to turn off Push and set Fetch to Manually.

Fetch options include the ability to:

- Turn Push on
- Set the interval to fetch data

MAIL

You can configure lots of Mail settings. You can add a signature to all outgoing e-mails (or change the current one), set the minimum font size for e-mail messages, set a default e-mail account, and more.

Mail options include the ability to:

- **Set the number of messages shown on the iPad**   You can opt to see the most recent 50, 100, 200, 500, or 1,000 messages.
- **Set how many lines of each message are previewed in the message list**   Change e-mail preview options, specifically, how many lines of text you'd like to preview (up to five).
- **Set a minimum font size for messages**   Set a font size, including Small, Medium, Large, Extra Large, or Giant.
- **Set whether iPad shows To and Cc labels in message lists**
- **Set whether iPad confirms that you want to delete a message**
- **Set whether iPad automatically loads remote images**   Loading remote images will cause the e-mail to take longer to load. You can manually load the images while reading the e-mail should you want to see them.

TIP

To change the sounds associated with Mail, in Settings, go to the General options, under Sounds.

- **Organize by thread** Have the iPad organize your e-mails by thread (conversation). A thread is created when you send e-mails back and forth to a person and the subject line remains the same.
- **Set whether iPad sends you a copy of every message you send** Send a blind carbon copy (Bcc) to yourself each time you send an e-mail.
- **Indent text when you forward or reply to a message** Tap Increase Quote Level to make the change.
- **Add a signature to your messages** Add, change, or delete the automatic signature for outgoing messages.
- **Set the default e-mail account** The default account is the one that will be used automatically each time you compose an e-mail and when you use other apps to send e-mail, like Maps or Photos.

To set an e-mail account as the default:

1. In the Settings app, tap **Mail, Contacts, Calendars**.

2. Scroll down and tap the arrow by **Default Account**.

3. Tap the account you want to use as the default.

CONTACTS

You can change how your contacts are sorted and displayed. For both, your choices are First, Last or Last, First. You can also add your own personal information and choose a default account for storing new contacts that are created outside of any specific account. What you add to My Info can be used by Safari to automatically fill in web forms.

CALENDAR

The Calendar helps you keep track of appointments and important dates. You can change how the Calendar sends you alerts, among other options.

To change the Calendar settings:

1. In the Settings app, tap **Mail, Contacts, Calendars**.

2. Scroll down to the **Calendars** section.

3. Tap to turn new invitation alerts on or off.

4. Tap the arrows by the other options to review and apply them (see Figure 10-7).

Figure 10-7: Calendar options are at the bottom of the Mail, Contacts, Calendars page.

10

Calendar options include the ability to:

- **Set alerts to sound when you receive meeting invitations**
- **Set how to use your current time zone**   Enable this to show event dates and times in the time zone selected for calendars.
- **Set how far back in the past to show your calendar events on iPad**
- **Set defaults for alert times**   Configure how early to be alerted, by default, for birthdays, events, and all-day events.
- **Choose a default calendar**   If you have more than one calendar configured on your iPad, you can set which of them is the default here.

REMINDERS

Here you configure how far back to sync reminders and what list (if you've created them) to use as the default.

Use Twitter

Twitter is a social networking application you can use to share short messages with others. Once you've installed and configured Twitter, you can configure how you'd like your iPad to use Twitter:

- **Manage your Twitter account**   Set what Twitter account name you'd like to use and enter your password. You can also enable or disable the option Find Me By Email to allow other people to follow/not follow you by searching for your e-mail. You can delete your account here, too, or add a second Twitter account.
- **Update your Contacts list with Twitter information**   Add Twitter user names and photos to your contact cards. When you tap Update Contacts, the update takes place.
- **Choose what apps can access your Twitter account**   Choose if Photos, Safari, and Twitter can use your account.

Set FaceTime Defaults

You'll use the FaceTime options to enable or disable FaceTime and to configure the account you want to use and the e-mail address associated with your account. You can also add another e-mail account if desired. There are only a couple of options, shown in Figure 10-8.

Figure 10-8: FaceTime can be enabled or disabled from Settings.

To change FaceTime settings:

1. In the Settings app, tap **FaceTime**.

2. To enable or disable FaceTime, tap **On** or **Off** (see Figure 10-8).

3. To add another e-mail address where you can be reached via FaceTime, tap **Add Another Email**, and fill out the information required.

Set Defaults for Safari

There are a few things you can configure regarding Safari. You can choose a specific search engine, enable AutoFill, always show the Bookmarks Bar, and more. For more information on using Safari, see Chapter 2.

GENERAL

General options include the ability to:

- **Select a search engine**   Options include Google, Yahoo!, and Bing.
- **Enable AutoFill**   Set Safari to automatically fill out web forms. Safari remembers data you've previously entered into webpages. It can also use information you define as My Info in the Mail, Contacts, Calendars category of Settings.
- **Opt to open new tabs in the background**   When a new tab is opened, it opens in the background when this is enabled. Otherwise, the new tab becomes the active tab.
- **Show the Bookmarks Bar**   When turned off, you can still reveal the Bookmarks Bar by clicking Safari's address bar or search box.

PRIVACY

Here you can make browsing with Safari a little bit more private:

- **Always browse with Private Browsing**   Enable this option to keep Safari from saving information about your browsing session, including cookies and history.
- **Accept or deny cookies**   Choose how to accept cookies from websites. Cookies are generally harmless and are what enable websites to greet you with personalized options, like your name or suggestions for what you may want to purchase.
- **Clear your history**
- **Clear your cookies and other data**

QUICKSTEPS

CHANGING YOUR SEARCH ENGINE

To change the search engine Safari uses by default:

1. Tap **Settings**.

2. Tap **Safari**.

3. Tap a new search engine.

4. Tap **Safari**.

SECURITY

Security options include the ability to:

- **Change security settings**   Turn Fraud Warning on or off; enable or disable JavaScript; block or allow pop-ups.
- **Configure advanced settings**   If you want to know when a webpage has errors, and if you're interested in resolving those errors because you develop apps or websites for the iPad, the debug console can help when this feature is turned on. You can also see what websites are storing data on your iPad.

Configure Messages

You configure how you want the Messages app to work here. iMessages can be sent between iPhones, iPads, and iPod touches. With the release of Mountain Lion in 2012, you'll also be able to communicate with Macs that run that OS.

From Messages you can

- **Enable or disable iMessages**   Turn the ability to use iMessages on or off.
- **Send read receipts**   Send read receipts for the iMessage you send.
- **Choose where to receive your messages**   Choose an e-mail address to receive iMessages.
- **Show or hide the subject field**   Show or hide the subject field in messages.

Configure Media Preferences

Media consists of music, videos, and photos. The Settings app offers three options for dealing with these: iPod, Videos, and Photos.

CONFIGURE MUSIC PREFERENCES

The Music app is the app you use to play music. You can configure various settings for the Music app, including playing all songs at the same sound level and setting a volume limit, among other things. See Figure 10-9.

The Music options include the ability to:

- **Turn on iTunes Match**   iTunes Match is a service you pay for that costs about $25 a year. With it you can store all of your music in iCloud and thus, access that music from all of your iDevices.

Figure 10-9: Consider enabling Home Sharing if you have a lot of media on your networked devices.

- **Set the Music app to play songs at the same sound level** Enable Sound Check.
- **Use EQ to customize the sound** Select an equalizer from a list of predefined settings.
- **Set a volume limit** Set the maximum volume and lock it, if desired.
- **Group by album artist** Group your music by the album artist, or not.
- **Home Sharing** Set up Home Sharing using your Apple ID and password. You'll need to enable Home Sharing in the same manner on your other iOS devices and in iTunes to get the most from it, and you can include up to five devices in any Home Sharing situation. Sharing will occur over your home Wi-Fi network, and you can then stream media from one device to another.

CONFIGURE VIDEO PREFERENCES

Video settings offer options that apply to all video content, including rented movies.

Video options include

- **Set where to resume playing** Set where videos that you previously started watching begin. You can resume playing from the beginning or where you left off.
- **Turn closed captioning on or off** To show or hide closed captions in video.
- **Home Sharing** Enable Home Sharing for videos across your home Wi-Fi network and other configured iDevices.

CONFIGURE PHOTOS PREFERENCES

Photos options include

- **Enable or disable Photo Stream** Set how to use Photo Stream. Photo Stream is what enables you to take a photo on your iPad and have it available on your other iDevices. It involves iCloud. All devices that you want to share should be configured to use Photo Stream.
- **Set the length of time each slide is shown in a slideshow** Specify the length of time each photo in a slideshow should appear before the next photo appears.
- **Set whether to repeat slideshows** Repeat slideshows once they finish playing.
- **Set photos to appear randomly or in order** Randomly shuffle photos in a slideshow.

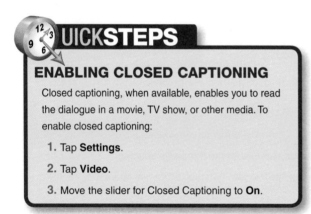

TIP

In iTunes, enable Home Sharing from the Advanced tab.

QUICKSTEPS

ENABLING CLOSED CAPTIONING

Closed captioning, when available, enables you to read the dialogue in a movie, TV show, or other media. To enable closed captioning:

1. Tap **Settings**.
2. Tap **Video**.
3. Move the slider for Closed Captioning to **On**.

CONFIGURING SETTINGS FOR ANY THIRD-PARTY APP

To configure settings for any third-party app:

1. Tap **Settings**.

2. Scroll down to the Apps section.

3. Tap any app.

4. Configure options as desired.

Set Notes Defaults

Tap any font to change the default font used for Notes. There are three: Noteworthy, Helvetica, and Market Felt. To create a note, tap **Notes** on the Home screen, and tap to begin typing. Notes will be saved automatically, and will appear in the left pane when in landscape view. Controls appear at the bottom of the screen. Notes will be saved automatically in the location that you configure for the default account.

Set Store Defaults

The Store settings offer a place to change or create an iTunes Store account.

Store options include

- **Enable or disable automatic downloads for music, apps, and books**   You can configure certain data to be downloaded automatically to your device, including music, apps, and books.

- **Use cellular data to download purchases (or not)**   When Wi-Fi isn't available and you want to make a purchase from the Store, enable this feature. This is only available on the cellular models of the iPad.
- **Automatically download new content when connected to Wi-Fi**   When you subscribe to a magazine, new content can be automatically delivered to your device when you're connected to Wi-Fi so you don't have to download it manually.
- **View your iTunes Store account information**   View information regarding your account, including your Apple ID, payment information, billing address, country or region, and more. You can manage your iTunes and iBookstore alerts here, manage subscriptions, and turn Genius on or off for apps. You can also delete your account. When you do, all Photo Stream photos and documents stored in iCloud will be deleted from your iPad.

Manage Apps

Apps you've acquired that offer settings options appear under the Apps section. What you see here will be specific to your iPad. Tap any app in the list to view the settings available. For more information about obtaining and using apps, refer to Chapter 6.

syncing
- apps, 8, 137
- audiobooks, 72
- bookmarks with info, 7
- books, 138–139
- calendars, 128
- calendars with info, 7
- contacts, 135–136
- contacts with info, 7
- data, 5
- defined, 134
- mail accounts, 137
- mail accounts with info, 7
- music files, 70–71
- music from specific artists, 73
- notes, 135–136
- notes with info, 7
- photos, 66–67
- playlists, 80
- podcasts, 73
- process of, 6
- selected music, 135–136
- videos, 66–67
- warning about, 10

T

tap-and-hold, described, 14
tapping, 15
Text Tone sound, playing, 17
texting, 114
.tiff extension, file type for, 47
time and date, setting, 163
touch techniques, 13
- creating Home screens, 14
- double-press, 14
- double-tap, 14
- flick, 14
- multitasking gestures, 15
- pinch, 14

tap-and-hold, 14
- using, 14–15
Track view, switching to Album Art
- view, 77
TV shows, obtaining from iTunes
- Store, 90
Tweet sound, playing, 17
Twitter, using, 169
.txt extension, file type for, 47

U

unlocking iPad, 18
updates, turning off, 25
updating iPad, 145
Usage options, accessing, 158

V

.vcf extension, file type for, 47
video chats, having with
- FaceTime, 67–68
video controls, using, 66
video preferences, configuring, 172
videos. See also YouTube
- Record button, 55–56
- sending via e-mail, 46
- syncing, 66–67
- taking, 55–56
Videos app
- features, 64
- finding videos, 65
- icon, 12
- Movies tab, 64
- playing videos, 65
- Podcasts tab, 64
- Store tab, 64
- TV Shows tab, 64
- using with iTunes U, 92

virtual keyboard
- displaying, 13
- hiding, 13
volume, adjusting, 76
Volume rocker, described, 10

W

wallpaper
- changing, 15–16, 155
- using photos for, 65
webpages
- saving as web clips, 30
- visiting in Safari, 26
websites
- Find My iPad, 19
- MobileMe migration to iCloud, 37
- podcasts, 74
Wi-Fi
- disabling, 151–152
- enabling, 151–152
- managing, 151–152
Wi-Fi + 4G, 22–23
Wi-Fi network
- connecting to, 23–24
- enabling, 24
- joining, 152
Wi-Fi only, 22–23
Wi-Fi Sync option, enabling, 160
wireless networks, viewing, 23

X

.xls/.xlsx extension, file type for, 47

Y

Yahoo! e-mail account, adding, 37–38
YouTube. See also videos

accessing videos, 106
adding videos to favorites, 107
commenting on videos, 108
controlling playback, 106
disliking videos, 107
Favorites button, 106
Featured button, 106
features, 105–106
flagging videos, 107
full-screen mode, 107
getting info about
- videos, 107
History button, 108
icon, 11
liking videos, 107
Most Viewed button, 106
My Videos button, 107
navigating videos, 107
pausing videos, 107
playing videos, 106–107
rating videos, 108
return to previous
- screen, 107
Search window, 107
searching for videos, 107
searching videos, 106–108
sharing videos, 107–109
Subscriptions button, 107
switching between
- modes, 106
switching categories, 107
Top Rated button, 106
uploading videos, 108
viewing comments, 107
viewing videos, 107
views, 107

Z

zooming in and out, 15